MODEL RAILROAD HANDBOOK NO. 28

BY ED HAMMER, LEE ZIES, AND MARC VAN CLEVEN

EDITOR: Jim Kelly
ART DIRECTOR: Vern Bleifuss
ARTISTS: Robert Wegner, Lee Vande Visse

The material in this book first appeared as articles in MODEL RAILROADER Magazine. The articles are reprinted in their entirety.

First printing, 1990. Second printing, 1995.

Published by Kalmbach Publishing Co., 21027 Crossroads Circle, P. O. Box 1612, Waukesha, WI 53187. Printed in U. S. A. Library of Congress Catalog Card Number: 90-62737. ISBN: 0-89024-119-8

Introducing the N scale Burlington Northern

A first look at our newest layout-building series

BY ED HAMMER

MODEL PHOTOS BY A. L. SCHMIDT

HOW DO you take the extensive system operated by the Burlington Northern RR and selectively compress it into an N scale layout that will fit into a 9 x 10-foot spare bedroom or den? After all, this system consists of 27,000 miles of track (making it the longest railroad in the country), along with more than 2,500 locomotives and 110,000 cars. That's the challenge the MODEL RAILROADER staff proposed to a group of N Scalers from nearby Madison, Wis., in late May of 1988.

HOW IT ALL BEGAN

The story as I have it is that MR wanted to try a new approach to building one of their project railroads. In the past they've built them themselves or worked with outside individuals, but this time they wanted to try working with a club or group. Also they wanted this project to be in N scale, as they hadn't done one in that small size since the Clinchfield, 12 years ago.

With that in mind, they asked Jim FitzGerald, N scale guru and editor of the *Ntrak Newsletter,* for his thoughts. After a week of rumination on his mountaintop in California, Jim recommended our Madison group, only 75 miles down the road from Milwaukee.

So associate editor Jim Kelly made a point of spying on us during an open house, held in conjunction with an NMRA division meet in late May of

Left: MR's newest project layout, the N scale Burlington Northern, actually features two railroads from opposite ends of the prototype spectrum. The Burlington Northern operates at high speed over a beautifully groomed double-track main line. The Wisconsin & Calumet, here represented by the blue GP9, is restricted to 10 mph on its run from Madison to Prairie du Chien.

Above: The scenic highlight on our N scale railroad is the BN's bridge across the Wisconsin River, just south of Prairie du Chien. Eagles soar along the bluffs high above.

Dick Christianson

"By the slough, by the slough, by the beautiful slough." The bank of the Mississipi River doesn't always run as straight as a railroad needs, so the line often crosses shallow backwaters on a fill, as seen here. Midway on the fill will be a short bridge, typically a concrete deck type, to accommodate the water's ebb and flow.

Right: What's this? Mountains in Wisconsin! Not really, but the 300- to 400-foot bluffs along the Mississippi River in the southwest corner of the state are beautiful and pretty impressive to midwestern flatlanders. Although Mike Danneman took this photo at Victory, a bit north of our modeled area, the scenery there is the same.

ROADWAY
BURLINGTON NORTHERN
3125
BURLINGTON NORTHERN
3147
NATIONAL

Cassville
Northern

The Denniston House in Cassville is a landmark hotel. Yes, the sign being half down is prototypical, although maybe they've fixed it by now. Kadee Lumber Co. is not affiliated with that Oregon bunch that makes all the beautiful N scale freight cars.

1988. MR, he said, was thinking about a modern Class 1 heavy-tonnage railroad that would absolutely have to fit in a 9 x 10-foot room.

One of our group suggested that the Wisconsin Central might meet the suggested guidelines. But those of you who know Jim realize that he already had the railroad and the general area selected. And the winner was — the Burlington Northern along the Mississippi River in southern Wisconsin. [Actually the locale was Wisconsin native Dick Christianson's idea. — *J. K.*]

A DINNER MEETING

A few weeks later we sat down at a restaurant midway between Milwaukee and Madison and over steak and orange roughy (to each his own) had a get-acquainted meeting with Russ Larson, Dick Christianson, and Jim Kelly. They took us on a slide tour of the area to be modeled and showed us a pencil sketch for the track plan. Also, they provided us with four rolls' worth of black-and-white photos depicting some of the typical scenes that Dick and Jim had found during a two-day "vacation" in the area.

After a lot of soul searching we got together in late June to iron out some last-minute questions and details. We had all thought about the time commitment for the project, but little did we realize the actual extent of that commitment, especially as it would affect ourselves and our families. Having finally crossed the line of no return, we wrapped up the details with MR — and away we went!

OFF AND RUNNING

Some people in the modeling group couldn't wait to get moving on the project, so they began taking field trips to the area before the final design was completed. Ostensibly, these trips enabled the persons involved to gather more firsthand information and details, material not included in the photos the MR staff had provided. Besides, it was great fun, and we got to breathe a little of that fresh air from the Coulee Region of Iowa, Minnesota, and Wisconsin.

Top left: The farthest point north represented on the layout is the huge 3M plant at Prairie du Chien. Cleaning products of all sorts are manufacturered here. The prototype is enormous and would overwhelm the layout if modeled actual scale size. As you might guess, this plant is the largest employer in the Prairie du Chien area. **Left:** The coal-burning electric power plant at Cassville is the southern-most point on the layout. Again, the prototype is a huge structure. The model representing it is large, but nowhere near scale-sized. Unfortunately for the railroad, the coal the plant receives is delivered by barges.

With a good deal of anticipation, the group got together again toward the end of July to review the final layout design, which Marc Van Cleven had completed using a computer-aided-design (CAD) program that's known as "Generic CADD." This is a low-cost software program, similar to "Autocad," and can be used with any IBM-PC compatible computer system.

Materials for the benchwork were ordered and delivered, and work began on the first Saturday of August 1988.

We set up a work schedule of Wednesday evenings and all day Saturdays through mid-July 1989, so that we could achieve the completion date. None of the fellows in our group had a spare bedroom, let alone a 9 x 10-foot room of any kind that was available when we started. Several of us, however, had basements that would accommodate the project at hand.

We initiated the "heavy-duty" cutting and assembly at Mike Vivion's home. By Labor Day 1988, the table assemblies were moved to my house, where the layout remained in residence until it was relocated to Milwaukee in late July of 1989 for photographing.

As the overall photo shows, the layout is "wrapped" by a 24"-high "skyboard," à la Ntrak. This is because we wanted the final product and the MR photos to reflect one of the project's original concepts — to make the layout look like it fits inside a 9 x 10-foot room.

FUDGING A LITTLE BIT

Had construction actually proceeded inside a room of the desired size, we would never have completed the project on time. At best, this is a one- or two-person construction operation if done solely from inside the benchwork. Note that three people can work from the inside, one on either side of the peninsula and one in the yard area. Don't try to move past each other, though, if one of you weighs more than 200 pounds!

We chose to make the layout portable, so we built it as six tables. One thought was that the individual tables could be taken home by as many as six people and completed there. Later, the tables could be brought together for a "show," similar in many respects to the modular railroading displays seen so often around the country. As it turned out, we could gainfully employ some five or six people at one time working on the project; fortunately, no more than that ever showed up at one time. It was difficult trying to keep one step ahead of the group in having enough modeling supplies available in a timely manner.

The structures were built by the fellows at their homes. Painting several of the buildings and figures was done at the home of one of our people, while most of the other work on the project was accomplished at the layout site.

As an aside, the basement corner used for the project was close to both a workbench and the furnace. The proximity of the workbench made it handy for many things besides tools, and the furnace was a necessity to have all winter long too. (It's often said that in Wisconsin we have nine months of winter and three months of tough sledding!)

THE CREW

Our group consisted of the following fellows from the Madison area: Bill Albert, Stan Graiewski, Curt Hammer, Ed Hammer, Rod Haushalter, Jack Hillebrandt, Ray Karnes, Steve Kellner, George Nelson, Marc Van Cleven, Mike Vivion, and Lee Zeis.

Because of varying job and family requirements, some of these people were unavailable for the scheduled work sessions but worked other times. Others volunteered their efforts towards the completion of one major part of the project. For example, Lee was principally responsible for the electrical design with help in the electrical installation facet of the project, while Ray was responsible for the backdrop painting.

THE LAYOUT EXPLORED

The layout attempts to represent the Burlington Northern's Chicago-Minneapolis double-track main line between milepost (MP) 213 at Cassville and MP 242 at Prairie du Chien (pronounced "prairie do sheen"), along the east bank of the Mississippi River. (For you purists, this is a part of the 4th Subdivision of the Chicago Division.) High traffic density, CTC (Centralized Traffic Control), and 75-mph speeds are the rule here. We're talking welded steel rail and a beautifully groomed, high-profile roadbed with ballast that looks like it should last a thousand years.

There's one bottleneck, though, and that's the single-track crossing of the Wisconsin River, about four miles south of Prairie du Chien. Most likely this bridge is a thorn in BN's paw, but it's great for a model railroad because it introduces some interesting and challenging operational possibilities. Two trains can't just orbit in opposite directions because they can't both be on the bridge at the same time — at least not for long.

Southwestern Wisconsin, where this segment of the prototype is located, lies in the unglaciated part of the state and so is much hillier, with bluffs 300 to 400 feet high rising steeply from the banks of the Mississippi. In some places, however, as at Prairie du Chien, the bluffs are set back roughly 1½ miles from the river's shoreline. These facts help to explain the rather abrupt vertical faces of the bluffs used on the layout.

It takes the form of a continuous, around-the-wall plan, with a center peninsula between Cassville and Prairie du Chien. There is a duckunder at an assumed "door" location on the "west" wall.

Starting on the southerly end in Cassville, some small local industries are served by the BN. The Nelson Dewey Power Plant is huge, but unfortunately not a big railroad customer. Its service trackage is used only when heavy equipment shipments (say transformers) are made. Barges deliver coal shipments to the power plant during the summer months.

The local industries in Cassville are represented on our layout by the Adrian Oil Co., the Kadee Lumber Co. (with a name like that, we N scalers just couldn't leave it out!), a feed mill and a warehouse. There's also the Denniston House, an 1836 hotel that's listed in the National Register of Historic Places.

Incidentally, the signs on the models

Dick Christianson

If the Prairie du Chien station could talk, it might reminisce about its heyday, when the *Twin Cities Zephyr* made flying stops on its rapid flights between Chicago and Minneapolis. The locomotive is a lease unit, one of 100 LMX B39-8s to be seen on the BN. LMX is a GE subsidiary and leases the locomotives to the railroad on a pay-per-power-used basis.

Our author, Ed Hammer, runs a train. We thank everyone in the Madison group and are especially grateful to Ed, who served as liaison between us and the Madison modelers. He ordered materials, kept the project on schedule, and even provided the basement where the layout was built! Ed is a colonel in the Army Reserve, and his leadership was just what this project needed.

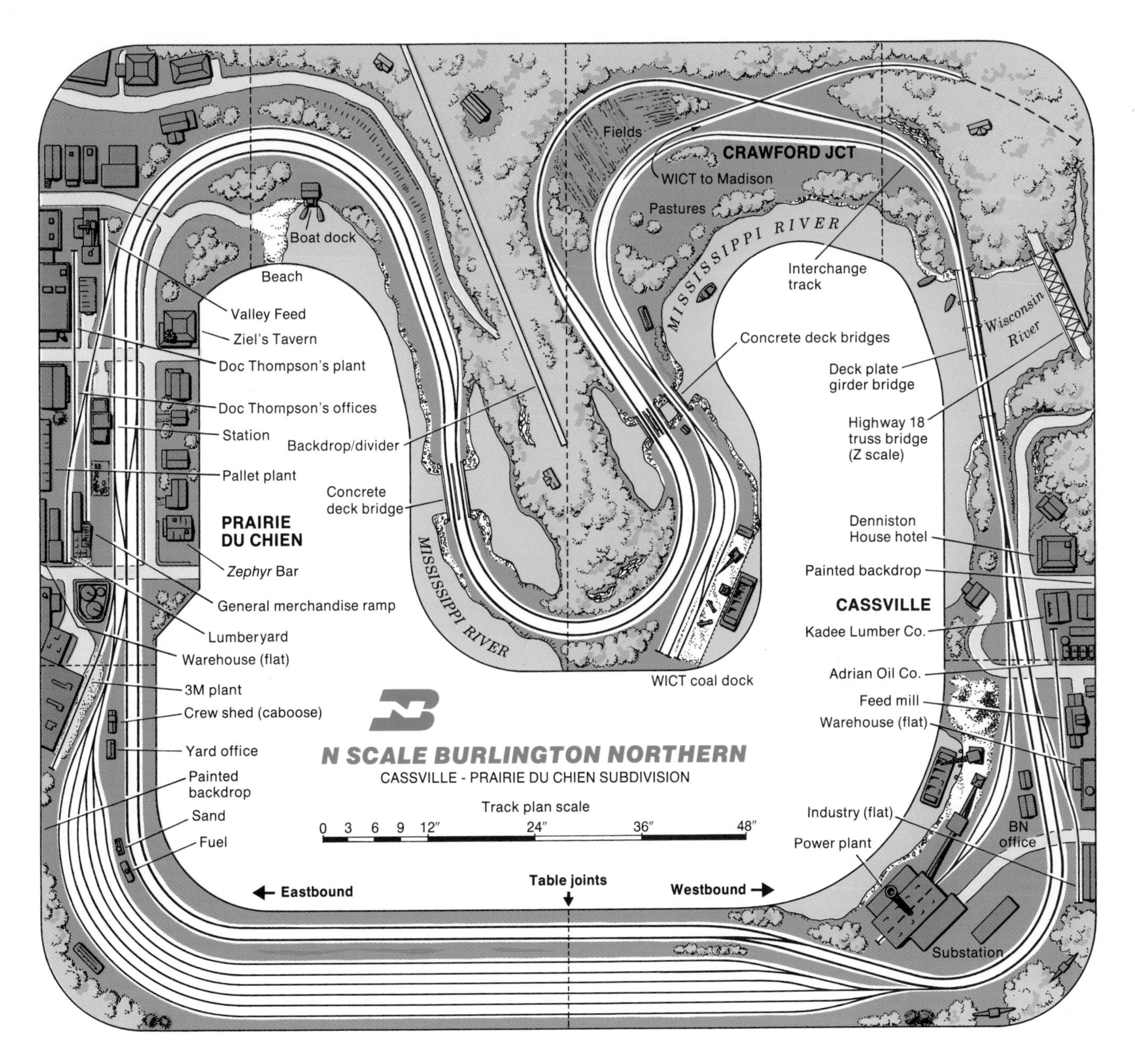

Mike Danneman

Here's the BN's Wisconsin River crossing as seen from high above at Wyalusing State Park (home incidentally to the state's largest population of bald eagles). The prototype bridge is more than 2,000 feet long. In the background is Prairie du Chien.

of the Kadee Lumber Co. and the Denniston House, as well as several other signs throughout the layout, are color photocopier reductions of the actual 35-mm color photos taken during one of my field trips.

THE BOTTLENECK

Shortly after leaving Cassville heading northbound, the double-track main converges to a single track before crossing the Wisconsin River. Our model bridge is comprised of several Micro-Engineering deck plate girder bridges, but its 240 scale feet is far short of the prototype's length of more than 2,000 feet.

The foot or so of trackage between Cassville and the Wisconsin River bridge is an extreme example of selective compression, representing about 20 miles on the prototype! We had to leave out the small communities of Glen Haven, Bagley, and Wyalusing.

About 1½ miles north of the Wisconsin River is Crawford Junction, where the Wisconsin & Calumet RR (locally called "the Wicket") crosses the Burlington Northern single-track main. This segment of the WICT, originating in Madison, is an old Milwaukee Road branch, and it serves some of the heavier tonnage customers in Prairie. Much of its traffic is off-loaded from barges plying the Mississippi River.

Interestingly, the track west of the junction, which appears to be a continuation of the WICT, is in fact owned by the BN, with the WICT having trackage rights. Interchange service between the two railroads is by a single-track connection at the junction. On our layout the WICT is represented by the coal docks in the center peninsula of the layout and the diamond at Crawford Junction. Our model WICT continues into hidden trackage behind the Wisconsin River, simulating a run to Madison.

Continuing northerly from Crawford Junction, the BN splits into a double main again while rumbling through some good croplands and continuing into Prairie du Chien.

Using a little modeler's license again, we introduced the crossing of several sloughs through this area. We simply didn't have enough room for them elsewhere on the layout. These types of sloughs are common throughout the region, but not in this particular area.

PRAIRIE DU CHIEN

Prairie du Chien is the largest river community between Dubuque, Iowa, and La Crosse, Wis., a distance of some 120 miles along the river's main channel. If you guessed that Prairie lies almost midway between those two larger communities, you would not be far from the truth. This, added to the fact that there's been a highway bridge over the Mississippi at Prairie for many years, means there's considerable more activity than we witnessed in Cassville, including rail service.

Prairie du Chien is home to a wide variety of rail-served industries, including the enormous 3M plant, two local feed warehouses, a lumberyard, and a general merchandise ramp.

Our trip around the layout ends at a modest, six-track yard that can be used for switching and a small amount of engine servicing. For timetable operation it doubles as an open "beyond the layout" staging yard serving both ends of the modeled stretch of line. A fair-sized yard lead is included, which allows the making or breaking of trains. Also the local switch engine to Prairie du Chien's industries works off this lead so as not to interfere with through operations on the main line.

On the prototype, mainline operations

BILL ALBERT
Bill is 45, married, and a building inspector for the city of Madison. He and his 8½-year-old daughter Katy are new to the hobby and are learning together while building a 4 x 8-foot N scale home layout. He did much of the scenery work on the BN layout.

STAN GRAIEWSKI
Stan, age 43, is married and works as an assessor for the city of Madison. He has a 32″ x 58″ N scale home layout and served as treasurer for the project, or as the group puts it, he laundered the money.

CURT HAMMER
Curt, our author's son, is 27 and a third-generation model railroader. He's a computer programmer and works for CUNA, a nationwide credit union. Among his many contributions to the BN layout was the kitbashed Denniston House at Cassville. Curt is a fan of the Great Northern and the Southern Pacific.

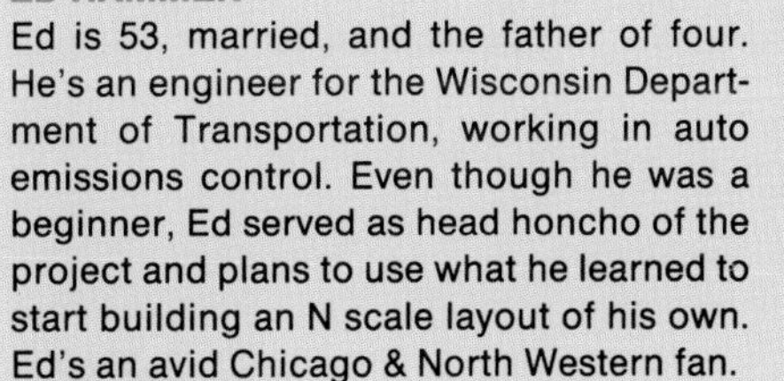

ED HAMMER
Ed is 53, married, and the father of four. He's an engineer for the Wisconsin Department of Transportation, working in auto emissions control. Even though he was a beginner, Ed served as head honcho of the project and plans to use what he learned to start building an N scale layout of his own. Ed's an avid Chicago & North Western fan.

ROD HAUSHALTER
Rod is a bus driver with the Madison Metro system. He's married, has a 3½-year-old son, and has been active in model railroading since the late 1950s and in N since the bad old days of Treble O. He plans to start soon on an Nn3 pike based on the White Pass & Yukon.

JACK HILLEBRANDT
Jack, age 71, brought 57 years of model railroading experience to the project. He's a retired engineer who worked for the Madison Gas & Electric Co. Many of the structures were scratchbuilt by Jack. He and his 9-year-old grandson, Andy Hornung, enjoy operating on Jack's C&NW home layout.

RAY KARNES
Ray, 34, is a cashier with the University of Wisconsin Credit Union. At home he models the Rock Island in N scale. His contribution to the project was painting the skyboards. Viewers marvel at how well his painted forest blends in with the lichen.

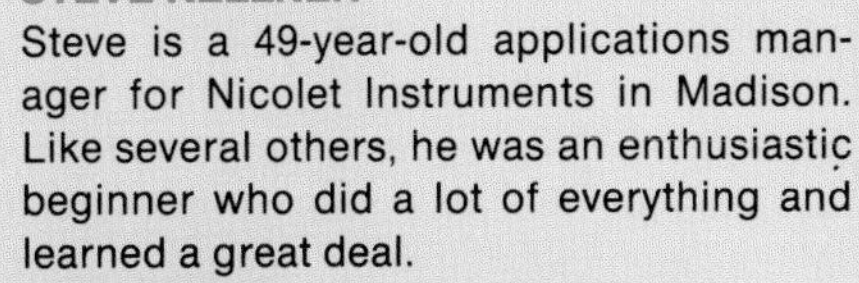

STEVE KELLNER
Steve is a 49-year-old applications manager for Nicolet Instruments in Madison. Like several others, he was an enthusiastic beginner who did a lot of everything and learned a great deal.

GEORGE NELSON
George, who works for the Dane County Maintenance Department, is 42, married, and the father of two daughters. He's a Burlington Northern fan through and through, so he felt like he'd been thrown in the briar patch when this project was proposed. George has an N scale BN layout at home and provided nearly all the locomotives and rolling stock used in our photos.

MARC VAN CLEVEN
Marc is 37, married, and has a 13-year-old daughter, Katie, who helps him paint structures and scenery. He's head electronics instructor at the Wisconsin School of Electronics in Madison. Marc finalized the layout's design using a computer. Among his other contributions were the Wisconsin River bridge and the 3M plant.

MIKE VIVION
Mike is 43 and married. He's a production manager with Nicolet Instruments, a Madison firm that manufactures medical instruments. His N scale home layout, the Marinette Valley & Santa Fe, is based on the Santa Fe. Like Jack Hillebrandt and Ed Hammer, he's also a circus train enthusiast and modeler.

LEE ZEISS
Lee is in charge of computer operations for RMT Inc., a Madison-based environmental consulting firm. He designed the layout's control system, wired the layout, and built the control panels, all the while working hard to complete an MBA at the University of Wisconsin.

are controlled by the BN operator via radio from Galesburg, Ill. The local switch engine makes a run down from La Crosse whenever the need arises.

Wisconsin & Calumet crossings of the BN main line at Crawford Junction are controlled by the BN operator in La Crosse; land line contact is made by the WICT crew both before and after crossing the diamond, using telephones that are located at the WICT derails on either side of the diamond.

Now you have a general idea of what this project railroad is all about. In the next several issues of MODEL RAILROADER, we'll take you through a series of "how-to" articles. We'll show you the challenges that we faced, how we resolved them, and the step-by-step procedures we followed in the construction of the Burlington Northern, Cassville-Prairie du Chien Subdivision.

See you next month! ♁

For a complete rundown on the river portion of the BN's Chicago Division, we recommend Gary Dolzall's article in the September 1988 issue of Trains Magazine.

Like to know more about the "Wicket"? Paul Swanson covered it in Trains *for July 1988.*

Track planning with a computer

Including tricks for making any layout look larger

BY MARC VAN CLEVEN
PHOTOS BY A. L. SCHMIDT

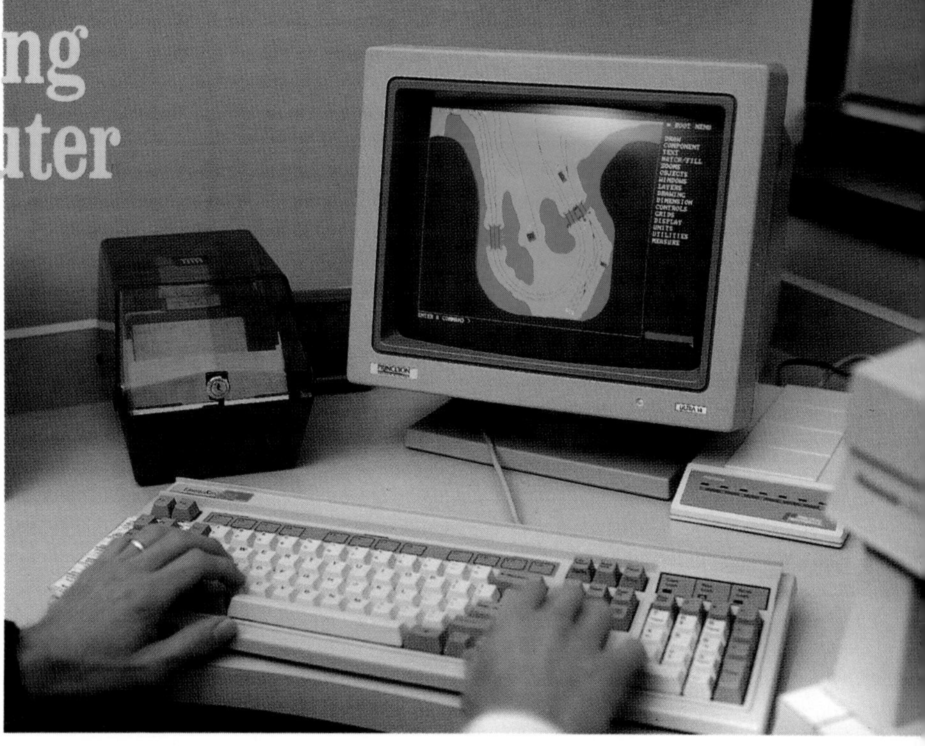

Our author used a computer to study, refine, and develop the BN track plan. Elements such as turnouts and curves can be stored in memory and inserted into the plan at will.

LAST MONTH we introduced our N scale Burlington Northern, a layout built for MODEL RAILROADER by a group of Madison, Wis., N scale modelers. The layout portrays the BN's double-track main line along the Mississippi River in southeastern Wisconsin.

To help us get started the MODEL RAILROADER staff gave us a rough track plan sketched in pencil, but it was up to us to make all the pieces fit and to work out the switching track arrangements in the towns. The MR people were adamant about not letting us push the walls of their theoretical 9 x 10-foot spare bedroom even a little farther apart. Our challenge was to create a serious-minded model railroader's first layout with the following restrictions:

- A minimum mainline radius of 12".
- All turnouts easily accessible.
- No hidden track.

COMPUTER DRAWING

I developed the final version of the track plan using an IBM-compatible personal computer and a computer-aided-design (CAD) software package called "Generic Cadd," by Generic Software Inc. These are powerful tools that make track planning a lot easier.

Using a computer you can draw the track plan quickly and accurately and make changes without having to redraw. See fig. 1. The track planner of yesteryear had a collection of turnout and curve templates, but today's designer has these components and more — such as crossings, crossovers, structures, etc. — stored in the computer's memory and available at the mere touch of a computer keyboard.

Nor do you have to worry about drawing in scale or using a scale rule. You just think and work in real feet and inches, and the computer will handle the conversions for you. Also, you can enlarge, or "zoom in," on a portion of the track plan for a closer look. Working on an enlarged version of a small section of the layout leads to greater accuracy of the drawing. When you want to see the entire plan on the screen, the program will size it for you automatically.

You can draw a track component, a turnout for example, full size, then call up as many as you want later, in any orientation, in whatever size you want.

I used an industrial plotter to draw this track plan in full size, but you shouldn't be discouraged if you don't have access to one. This CAD has a utility program that turns your dot-matrix printer into a plotter for producing crisp, high-resolution drawings to whatever size you want. The program can be used with hundreds of printers, including color and laser types.

FIELD RESEARCH

Achieving continuity from one scene to another called for some field research, known otherwise as railfanning. You need to get a sense of a railroad's surroundings, especially with N scale. Many of the finest N scale layouts in the country portray the panorama surrounding the railroad as well as the immediate railroad scene, a perspective not routinely enjoyed by larger scales!

Plotting the industries in Cassville and Prairie du Chien was done on location, with copies of the layout sketch in hand. We decided to depict the industrial sidings as accurately as possible and avoid the temptation to create complicated switching puzzles. Following prototype makes the track plan less complicated and enhances the operation, particularly as our model trains have such short main lines to run on.

Let's go counterclockwise around the railroad, starting at Cassville. We discovered that the power plant siding is used solely for flatcars carrying large, bulky machinery and equipment such as generators and transformers. All coal deliveries come by barge to the plant. Also in Cassville is a siding serving four industries.

West of Cassville, the BN becomes a single-track main line approaching the Wisconsin River bridge. The real bridge is more than 2,000 feet long, but after many attempts at including a longer bridge, we found that the greatest scale length we could attain at this site while maintaining the minimum mainline radius of 12" was 240 feet.

Micro Engineering's great-looking deck girder bridges seemed the obvious starting point for this structure, and as I've used them in other plans they were already developed as components in the CAD program. Based on photos of the bridge, I decided that its character could be best recognized by using four

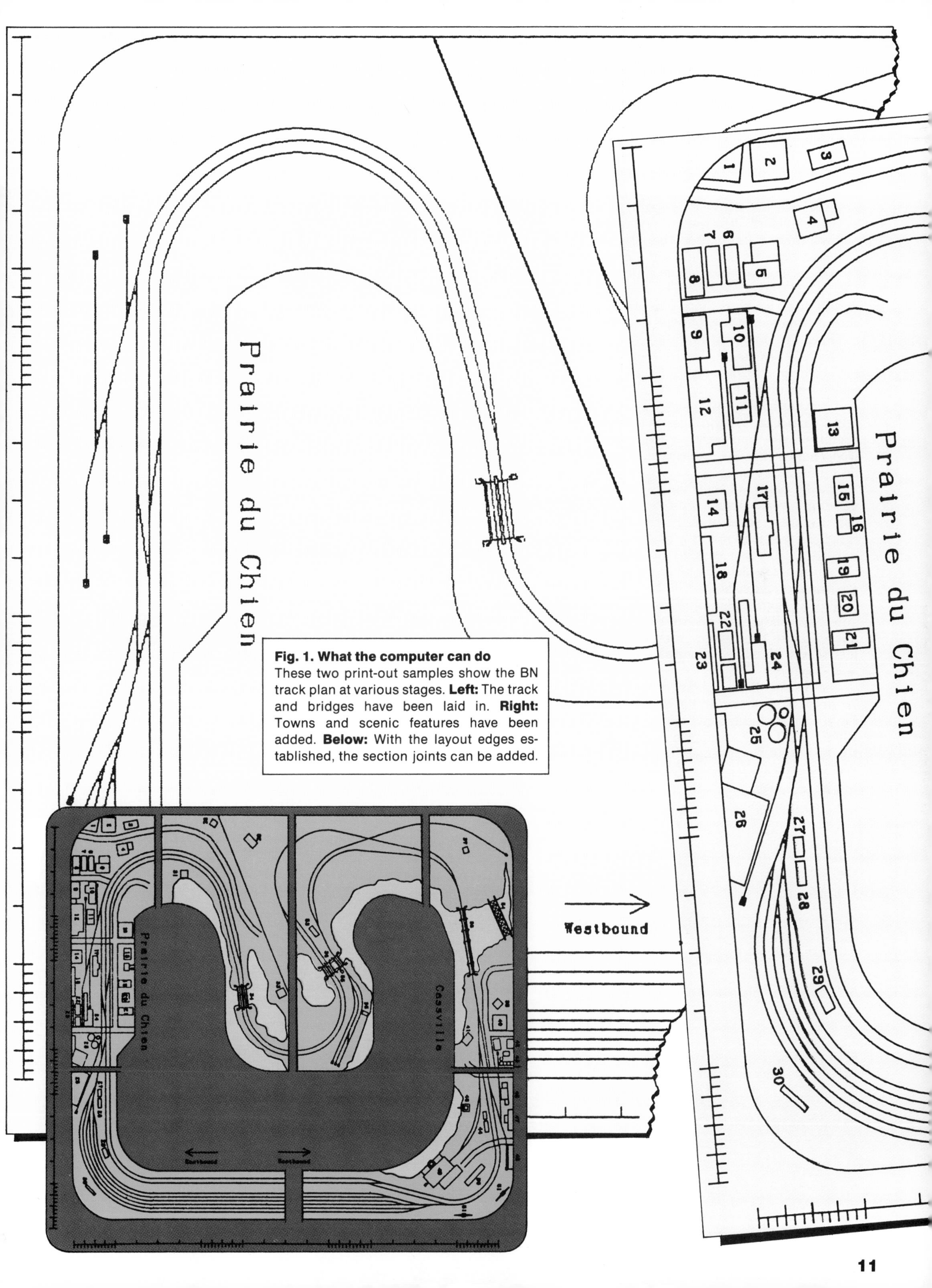

Fig. 1. What the computer can do
These two print-out samples show the BN track plan at various stages. **Left:** The track and bridges have been laid in. **Right:** Towns and scenic features have been added. **Below:** With the layout edges established, the section joints can be added.

40-foot spans and one 80-footer. I also had to be sure to place the single-track Burlington Northern main line out toward the aisle to allow the Wisconsin River room enough to curve away from the viewer and disappear.

The U. S. Highway 18 bridge is only a few inches behind the BN bridge. To make it look farther away this bridge is in Z scale, as are the vehicles on it.

The Crawford Junction interchange follows immediately after the bridge. The prototype BN main line is protected by derails on the Wisconsin & Calumet RR (WICT) track. Peco offers working derailers, so we used those to represent the ones found on the prototype.

There are only two mainline tracks at the real Prairie du Chien depot. But for better operation and switching we added a third track going through town and serving both as an industrial siding and a yard lead. The sidings are located prototypically and serve a feed mill, Doc Thompson's, a lumberyard, a pallet plant, and a ramp.

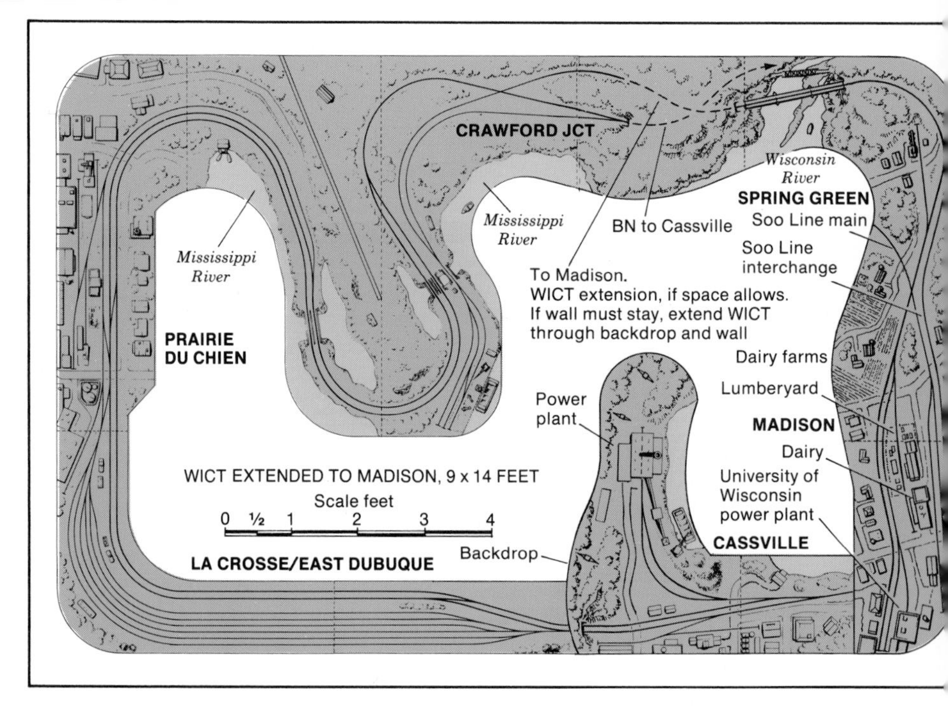

The 3M plant, a large facility encompassing several acres, consists of several separate structures. In the plan, this facility serves not only as a siding, but also visually separates Prairie du Chien from the double-ended six-track staging/storage yard.

This layout is designed to break down into six pieces. Should there be a need to ship the layout in crates, the pieces can be paired according to size and shape.

The N scale BN has plenty of potential for growth, as shown in fig. 2. Not only could you expand the BN main, but the WICT main line disappearing behind the hill could be continued through the backdrop to connect with either a reversing loop or a terminal remote from the layout, perhaps even in another room. Madison would be a natural choice.

DESIGN PRINCIPLES

The design device we used most often was the "channeling effect." See fig. 3. Simply stated, the idea is to draw the viewer's eyes to the center of the scene by concentrating interest and detail there. Transition areas should remain neutral, nicely done, but with nothing special to draw the eye. At Cassville, for example, the viewer's attention is focused left of the power plant and right of the large bluff. Both the bluff and the power plant frame the town and channel the view toward the center.

Another rule of thumb was to "break the train," basically by making sure there were some structures and scenery features between the viewer and the train. This technique makes both the railroad and the train seem longer.

Turning to Cassville again, the power plant is positioned to visually separate the six-track yard from the town of Cassville. It also breaks the view of the main line.

We found it vital to "extend the scenery beyond the backdrop." At the Wisconsin River bridge, for example, it was essential to prevent the view of the river from ending at the backdrop. Rather, we bent the river away from the viewer and behind the hill.

The Z scale U. S. Highway 18 bridge is one example of forced perspective; the heights of the various bluffs are others. Those closest to the main line are higher than those farther away. We applied this technique to both modeled and painted bluffs. Also, we used the finest tufts of lichen on the hilltops farthest away to make them look even farther. Houses and barns far in from the track or atop the bluffs are Z scale.

To take the WICT off-stage, we led it behind the same hill that hides the end of the Wisconsin River. There's enough track back there to hide a five- or six-car freight train, yet it's easily accessible to the operator.

In Prairie du Chien, another technique, "taking the train away from the edge," allowed us to build up the scenes on both sides of the tracks and really capture the town's character. The overall scene — the station, taverns, industries,

Ed Hammer tries on the N scale Burlington Northern for size. The 9 x 10-foot walkaround layout accommodates two operators easily. The river bluffs are perfect for a backdrop.

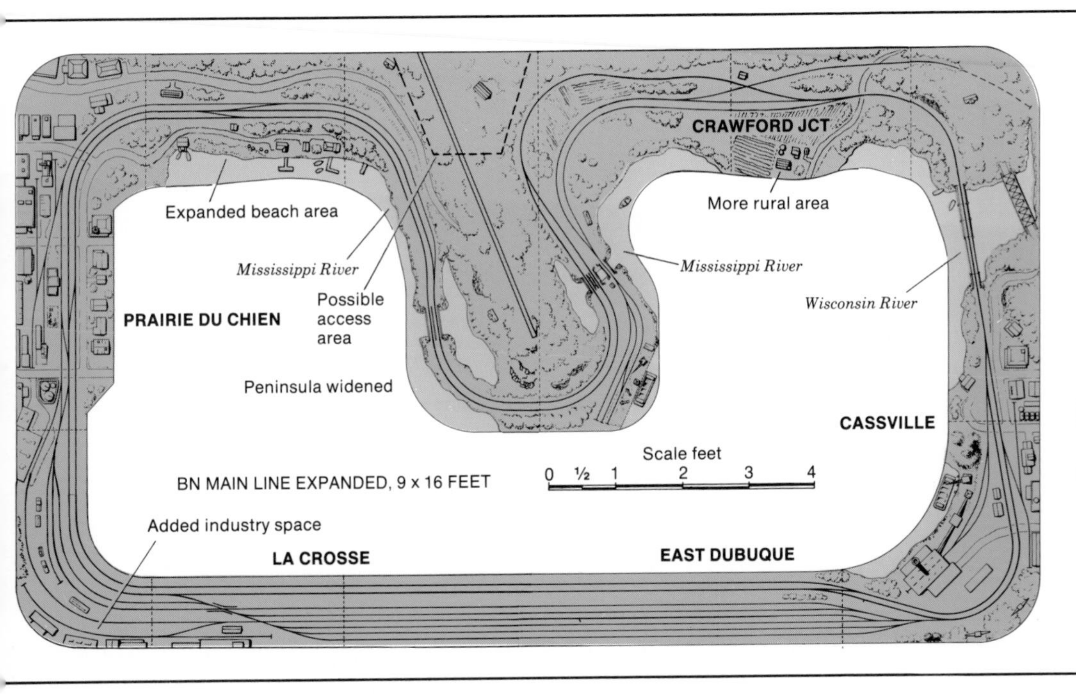

Fig. 2

EXPANDING THE BURLINGTON NORTHERN

and human activity — becomes the focus of attention. Again, the buildings and trees in the foreground break up our views of the trains and make them seem longer.

We couldn't find perfect solutions to all the scenery problems. Take town streets terminating against the backdrop, for example. Whenever possible we hid the abrupt ends of the streets with structures and building flats. When we couldn't do that we simply painted the continuation of the street onto the backdrop. Roads out in the countryside disappear into cuts in the bluffs.

Our bluffs had to be much steeper than the real thing just so we'd have some room left for a railroad. This called for compromises, but turned out not to be too tough a problem. Along the rear wall the bluffs are virtually vertical, but there's no place where a viewer can situate himself to sight along them. Where slope can be detected slope exists, and at the town sites the bluffs are simply painted on the backdrop.

As I said toward the beginning of this article, the tools and techniques of layout design have changed. Now we have the computer and CAD software to make the drawing easier. And don't forget that books and articles by our best layout designers, John Armstrong in particular, are available. All this makes it possible for the average modeler, with time and research, to design an accurate representation of a big railroad in a small space and have lots of fun doing it.

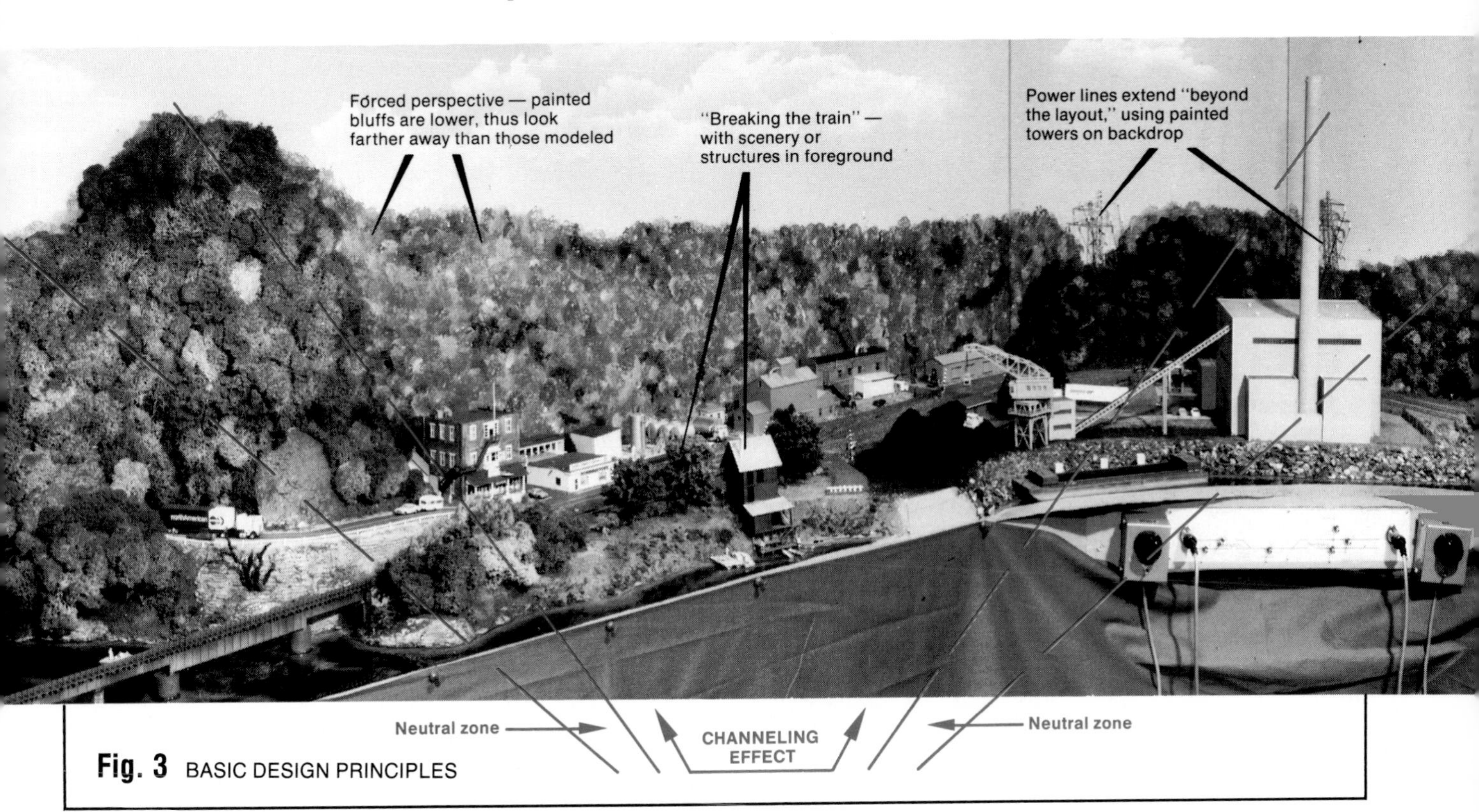

Fig. 3 BASIC DESIGN PRINCIPLES

Benchwork for the N scale Burlington Northern

Our project railroad was built in six lightweight sections for easy moving

BY ED HAMMER
PHOTOS BY THE BN BUILDERS

OVER THE last two months, we've introduced you to MODEL RAILROADER's N scale Burlington Northern railroad. This month we'll start building the layout. Some of you may already be revving up your saber saws, so let's go!

BUILDING THE TABLETOPS

First you need to buy your materials — your shopping list is included in fig. 1. It's a good idea to add an extra 10 percent to your lumber order to make up for warpage, cutting errors, and waste. It's another good idea to hand-select the wood. We ordered ours for delivery from one of the local lumberyards, so we weren't able to.

Before cutting anything be sure to look over the wood closely, so as to work around any knots, splits, warpage, and so on. Then sort, mark, and cut the various members. See fig. 2. Don't assume that any of the ends are square. Check them and then recut as is necessary.

This is open-grid style benchwork requiring butt joints, so the cuts need to be accurate and square. We used a Shopsmith (a multi-purpose stationary motorized power tool) for all the cutting and most of the drilling, but there are a variety of ways you could saw the wood. You could use a radial arm saw or a table saw to get good, square cuts. Failing that, there's still the good old miter box and miter handsaw. These will do just as good a job and won't take that much longer.

For rough trimming you can use a power circular saw, band saw, jigsaw, or saber saw. And again, the good, old-fashioned crosscut handsaw is more than up to the job.

Don't forget that safety is paramount when operating power tools, so wear safety goggles. Also remember to watch your fingers so they don't get in the way of a sharp blade.

As we cut the basic 1 x 4 framing pieces, we trial-fit them together and carefully labeled the parts for each of the six tables. Then we put them in separate piles.

Working on a concrete basement floor, we assembled the six basic benchwork units with yellow carpenter's glue and "all-purpose screws," as shown in fig. 3. The latter, also known as "drywall screws," are available in several lengths

Left: Just to keep you motivated while building benchwork, here's a shot taken on the finished layout. We introduced the N scale Burlington Northern in our February issue. It's a 9 x 10-foot layout based on the BN's double-track main line along the Mississippi River in southeastern Wisconsin. Here a freight zips through Prairie du Chien. Across the street is the *Zephyr* Bar, named for the Burlington RR's great passenger trains of the 1950s.

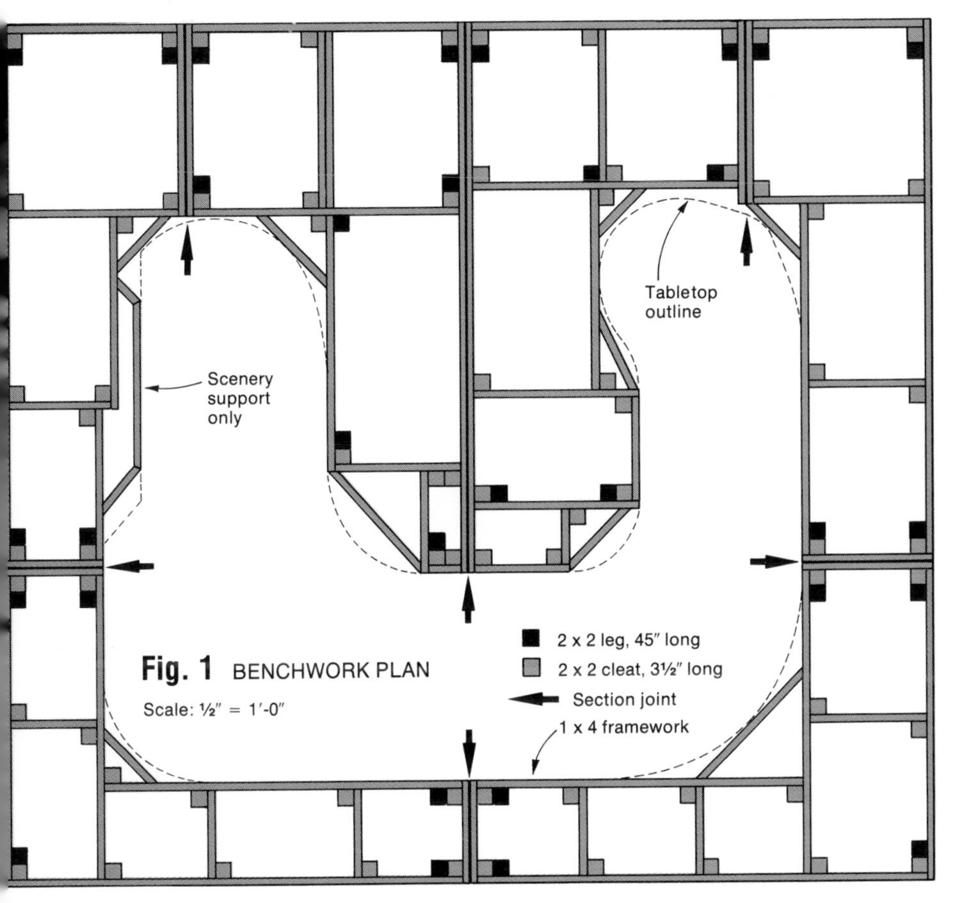

Fig. 1 BENCHWORK PLAN

Scale: ½" = 1'-0"

FIG. 2. CUTTING THE FRAMING

Top: Our builders double-checked each board end for squareness. **Above:** The pieces were carefully cut to length. **Below:** Note the use of safety glasses and a clamping device for sawing short lengths of 2 x 2.

and come with a Phillips head. You could also use regular, flathead wood screws, being sure to drill pilot holes for them.

We braced the corners with 3½" lengths of 2 x 2. In this less-than-perfect world our 1 x 4 framing material varied in depth from 3½" to 3⅝". We did not bother to trim it all to one size, although some people might insist that this ought to be done.

ADDING THE LEGS

Next, we cut the 45"-long 2 x 2 legs and installed leveling bolt feet as shown in fig. 4. Here's a little trick for installing the tee nuts that hold the leveling bolts: Screw the bolts into the tee nuts until only about 1" of thread remains above the nut. Insert this assembly into the leg hole, then seat the tee nut by tapping the bolt with a hammer, thus aligning the tee nut with the hole.

Before I forget, the 45" leg length places the top of the roadbed at 46⅞" from the floor. We were striving for a 49" benchwork height, but the ceiling in my basement necessitated staying a little lower. Even so, in one place we

Bill of materials

Hardware
- 1½" drywall screws (5 pounds)
- 5/16" x 2" carriage bolts (15)
- 5/16" x 3" carriage bolts (36)
- 5/16" washers (51)
- 5/16" hex nuts (51)
- ⅜" x 4" tap bolts for leg levelers (24)
- ⅜"-16 tee nuts for tap bolts (24)
- ⅝" x 4" mending plates (16)

Homasote
- ½" x 4' x 8' for subroadbed (2 sheets)

Lumber
- ⅜" x 4' x 8' AC plywood for tabletops and skyboards (6 sheets)
- 1" x 2" x 8' for leg bracing (14 pieces)
- 1" x 4" x 8' for framing (20 pieces)
- 2" x 2" x 10' for legs and cleats (16 pieces)

Styrofoam
- 1" x 4' x 8' for tabletop and scenery (5 sheets)
- 2" x 4' x 8' for scenery (2 sheets)

Miscellaneous
- Carpenter's glue (5 16-ounce bottles)
- Sandpaper (coarse, medium, fine)

FIG. 3. ASSEMBLING THE TABLETOPS
Left: Our builders used 1 x 4 framing with 2 x 2 corner braces. A few finishing nails hold this diagonal piece until screws can be driven. **Middle:** Drywall screws were used throughout the construction, driven with a bit in a variable-speed electric drill. **Right:** Here four of the six sections have been trial-fit together.

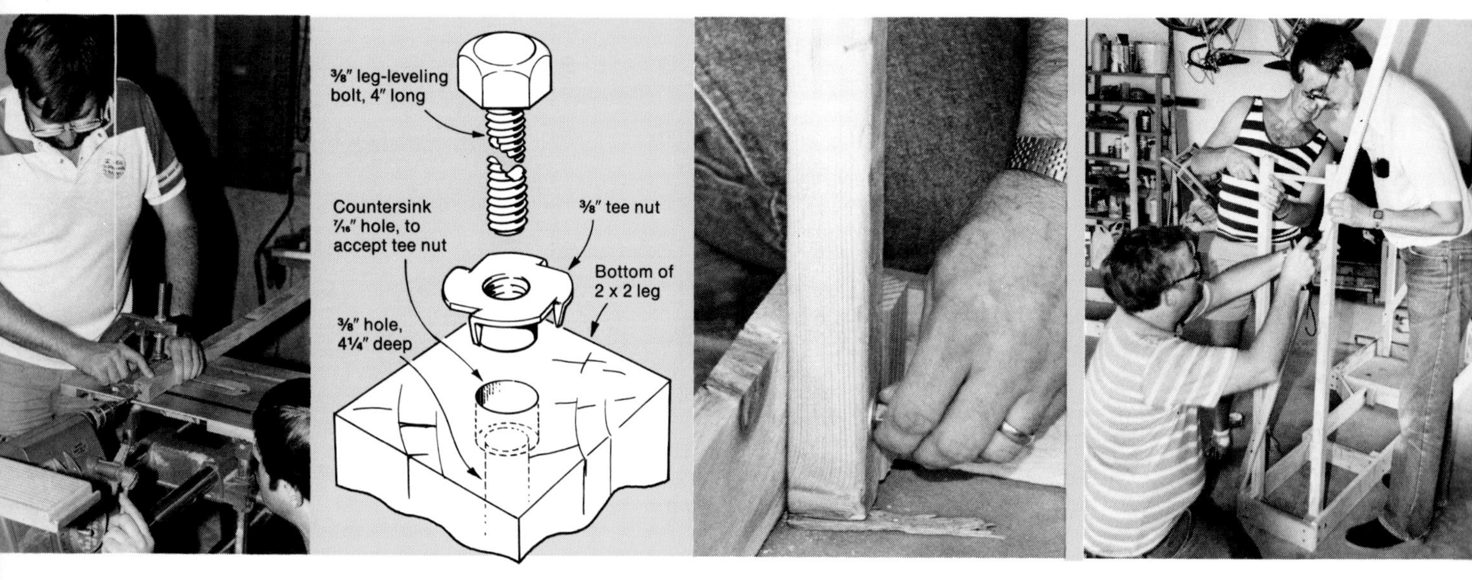

FIG. 4. CONSTRUCTING THE LEGS
Left: Holes were drilled in the ends of the legs to accept the tee nuts. **Above:** Legs were bolted to the tabletops. **Right:** Diagonal braces were trimmed flush after screwing them to the legs.

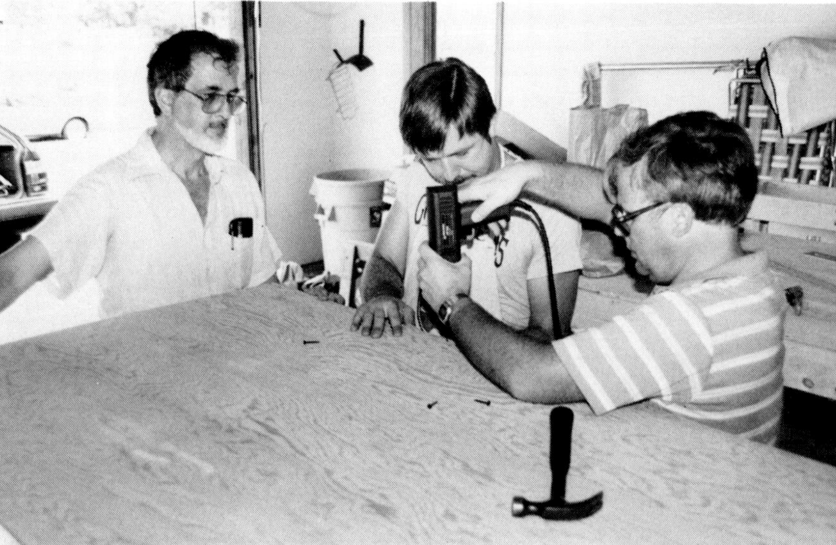

FIG. 5. ADDING THE TABLETOPS
Above: A steel straightedge ensured good, straight cuts on the plywood tops so the tables would butt tightly together. **Right:** The plywood tops were fastened down with drywall screws. **Far right:** The crew trimmed the curved edges to their final contours after the plywood tops were fastened down.

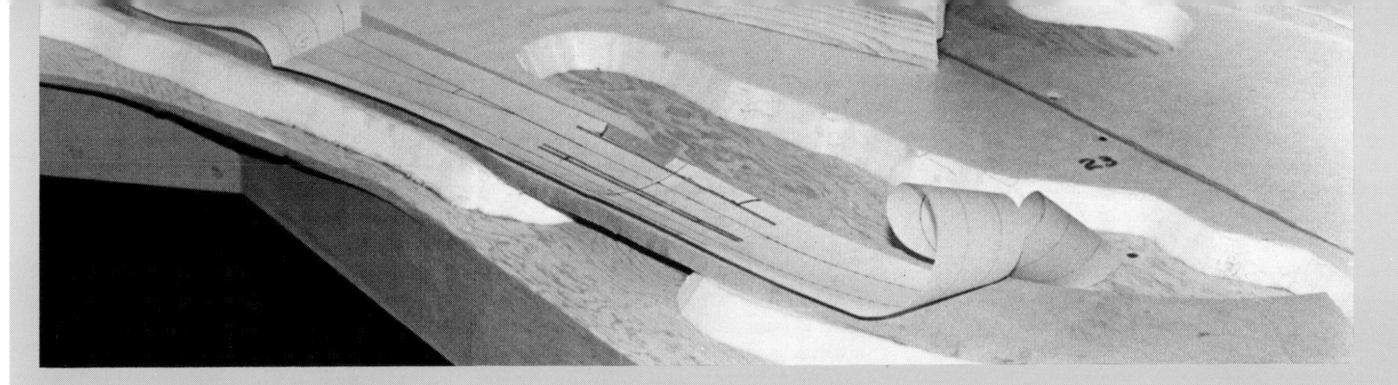

FIG. 6. FOAM/HOMASOTE SANDWICH
Above: All land area received a layer of 1″ Styrofoam. Track areas received an additional ½″ of Homasote, a pressed paper product that holds track nails well. **Below left:** Styrofoam banks along the river were cut at an angle with a saber saw. **Bottom left:** The plywood top guided the saw when cutting foam along curved edges.

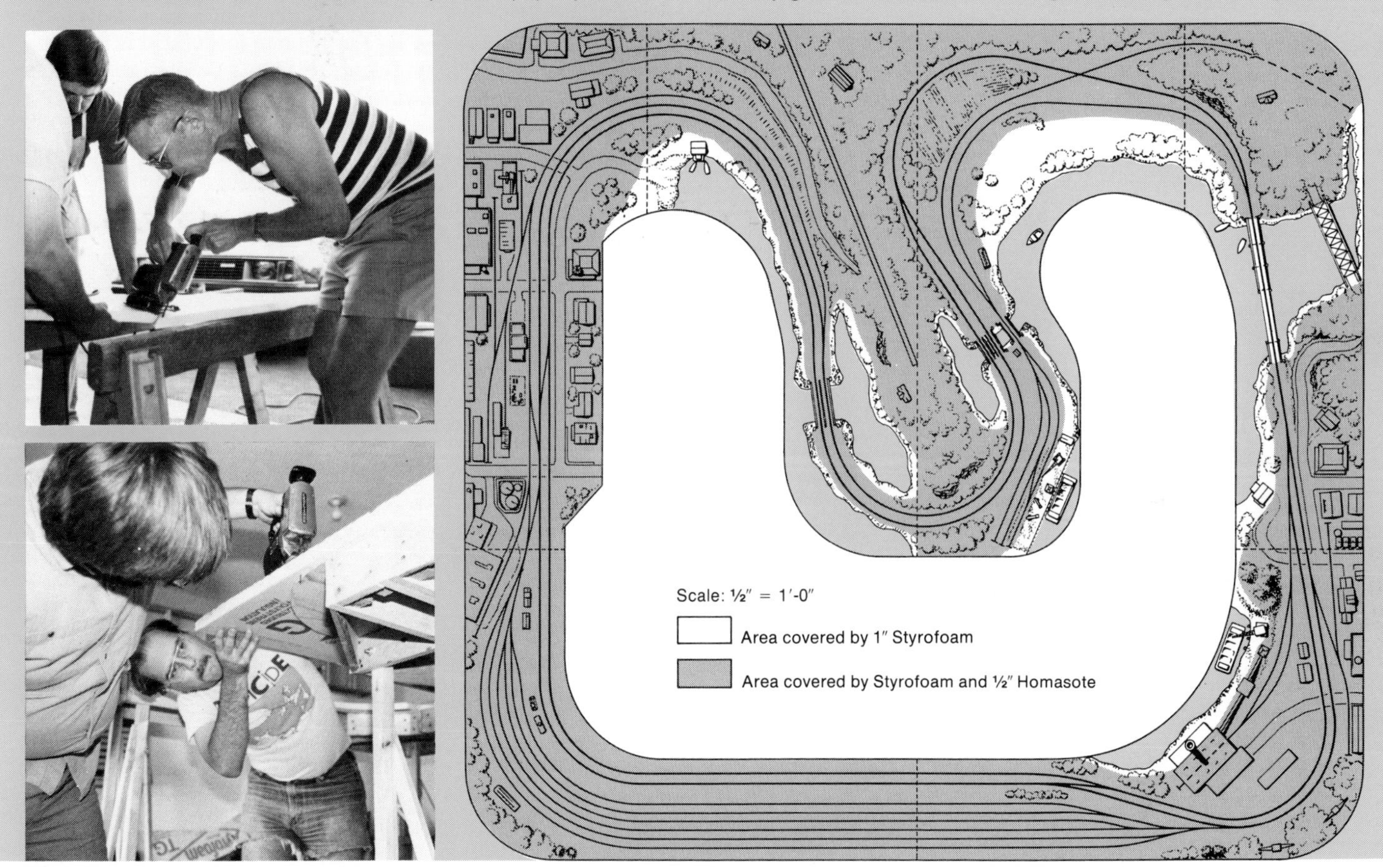

ended up with only 1½″ of clearance between the skyboards and the ceiling-mounted fluorescent lights.

For our next work session we moved out to the garage to enjoy some fine summer weather. We mounted the legs to the tables with carriage bolts, then attached 1 x 2 diagonal bracing. Before running in the drywall screws we made sure the legs were square to the table, using a square rather than a level, as the garage floor we were working on was pitched.

As shown in fig. 4, we trimmed the leg braces after they were attached, as this was a lot easier than trying to calculate and precut the angle. For extra stability we inserted a short piece of 2 x 2 between the diagonal braces where they crossed. We secured this piece with drywall screws.

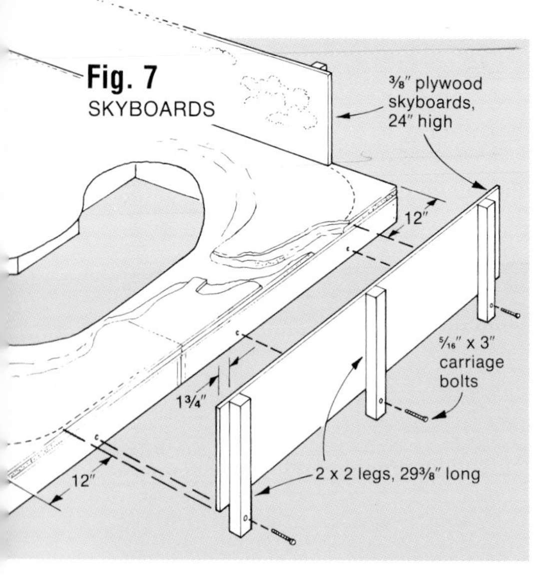

PLYWOOD TOPS

The next order of business was cutting and trimming the 3/8″ AC plywood for the tabletops, as shown in fig. 5. We used our full-size computer-drawn templates for this, but you could simply use the finished frames and the track plan as a guide for drawing yours.

We made certain as we went along that the plywood tops of adjoining sections would meet at right angles. Then we fastened them to the tabletops with drywall screws.

Now came the big moment, bolting the individual tables together. Even though we'd been careful throughout, one side of the layout came out 1/4″ longer than the other! Using a belt sander we ground away at two adjacent vertical faces until the entire tabletop became rectangular at 9 x 10 feet. Then we bolted the tables together with 2″ carriage bolts, washers, and hex nuts.

CHANGE OF PLAN

Our original plan had been to let the plywood tabletops represent the water surface, to which we would add 1/2″ of Homasote for the "land." But it became painfully clear that this idea wasn't going to work — the track wouldn't be high enough above the water. The Wisconsin River bridge, in particular, just wasn't going to work out.

To get more clearance we added a layer of 1″ Styrofoam in the land areas directly on top of the plywood. Then we covered the Styrofoam with the Homasote, as

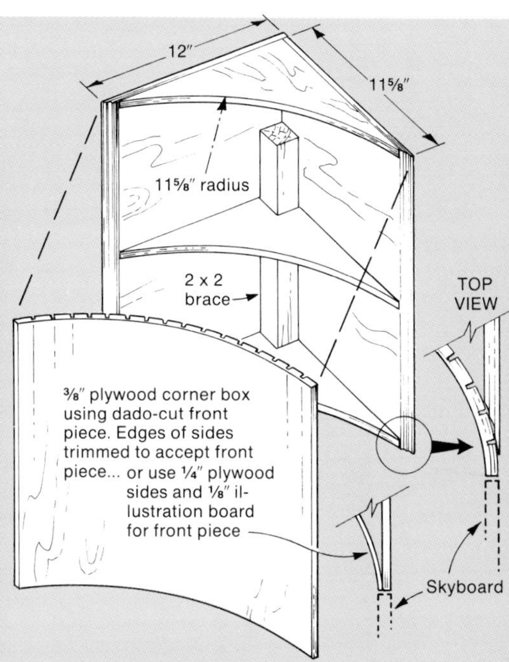

FIG. 8. BUILDING THE CORNER BOXES

Above left: Plywood corner boxes were faced with 3/8″ plywood, grooved along the back so it would bend enough. **Above right:** Plenty of glue was applied to hold the edges. **Far left:** The sides of the curved portions were nailed down. **Left:** The ends were clamped firmly until the glue set. **Below:** Mounting blocks cut from 1 x 4 were added for attaching the corner boxes to the skyboards.

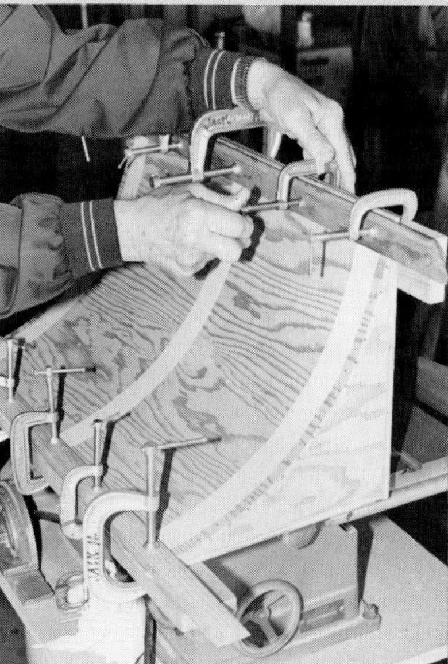

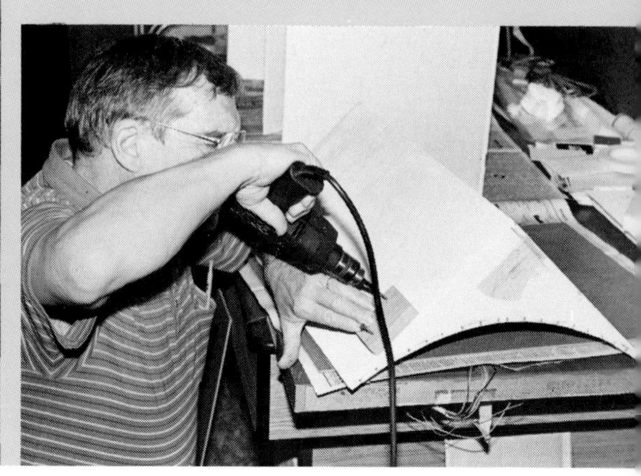

shown in fig. 6. We used yellow carpenter's glue between each of the layers and drove 20 penny nails through the three layers of the "sandwich" into the 1 x 4 framing.

Since 1" equals approximately 13⅓ N scale feet, we had achieved a vertical clearance of some 20 feet from water level to the top of the track, which is about right for the prototype in this area. One shortcoming, though, was that the model river embankments turned out steeper than they are in real life.

SKYBOARDS

Cutting and assembling the ⅜" plywood "skyboards" was straightforward, except for one teeny-weeny little detail I'll get to later. Two of the 24"-wide skyboards are 7 feet long, and the other two measure 8 feet. Figure 7 shows the "legs" that were attached for mounting these panels to the layout. Remember, if you are actually building the layout in a layout room, you don't need skyboards at all — you've already got walls!

After the glue had dried, we centered each of the four long skyboards on their respective sides of the layout. Then we drilled 5/16" holes through each of the three 2 x 2 skyboard legs and on through the 1 x 4 benchwork framing. We secured the skyboards with carriage bolts.

It's a good idea to label each skyboard and the corresponding benchwork with some key to aid in later assembly. We selected the rather original words of North, East, South, and West. Since Prairie du Chien is north of Cassville, it was called North, the yard became West, etc. Don't knock it, it worked.

The skyboard for the center peninsula is a 48"-long piece of ⅜" AC plywood whose finished height matches the other skyboards. It's easily removable and held in position with a simple channel made by nailing 1 x 2s to each side on the tabletops.

One last thought about this channel — it is cut where it crosses the table joint. Part of this channel goes with each of the peninsula tables when they are moved. The skyboard is held vertical between a pair of cleats attached to the rear skyboard.

CORNER BOXES

If you've gotten this far, you will note that the four corners do not yet have any skyboard treatment! This is that one "small detail" I mentioned a few paragraphs back. Figure 8 shows how we built our four corner boxes.

Before starting, carefully measure from the end of each skyboard to each corner on the layout. If you've done a good job or gotten lucky, the distance on each should be 12". Any place where it isn't, you'll either have to make a special corner to fit or else trim or adjust the skyboard. The latter would be easier.

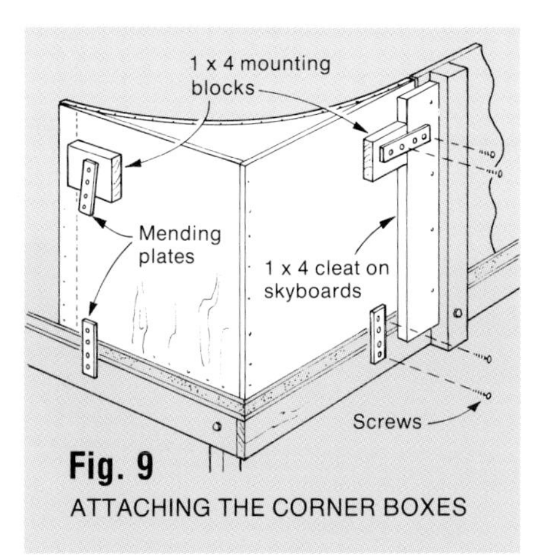

Fig. 9
ATTACHING THE CORNER BOXES

To make a corner box, cut the two sides first, then glue and screw them together. Next, cut and install the three "shelves" that brace the corner.

Now for the coup de grace! Another piece of plywood, 17¾" x 24", is cut to make the curved surface. That length can be found mathematically, or we can simply measure along one of the curved cuts made earlier. Then, use a table saw or circular saw to dado the back side of this latter piece of plywood so that only thin strips of the first ply hold the entire piece together. When we held these panels up against the sun, we could see light through the slits — now that's thin!

Glue and tack these curving pieces to the frame, and there's your corner box. You can probably build one faster than I can write about it — try it.

[Those of you unequipped to dado (cut grooves) in the back of the panel, might consider using illustration board as an alternative, as also shown in fig. 8. This should also solve the problem with painting, discussed next. — *Ed.*]

Painting the corner boxes was not without its perils. That thin strip of plywood "bubbled up," a challenge we met by applying a layer of "self-adhesive glass mesh patch/joint tape." Pro Mesh was the brand name. Over that joint tape, we added three or four layers of Ready Patch spackling compound. These or similar products should be available at hardware or building supply stores.

Build each of these corner boxes to fit its specific location. You would do well to mark them in a manner similar to your marking of the skyboards, using such words as Northeast, Southeast, Southwest, and Northwest. Catchy, isn't it?

To hold the corner boxes in position and to tighten the entire skyboard system, we used ⅝" x 4" metal mending plates from the hardware store (fig. 9).

The dirty work behind us, we took the layout apart and moved it into my basement, where we'd spend the winter completing it. See fig. 10. Next month we'll lay the cork roadbed, rough in the scenery, and lay the track. See you then!

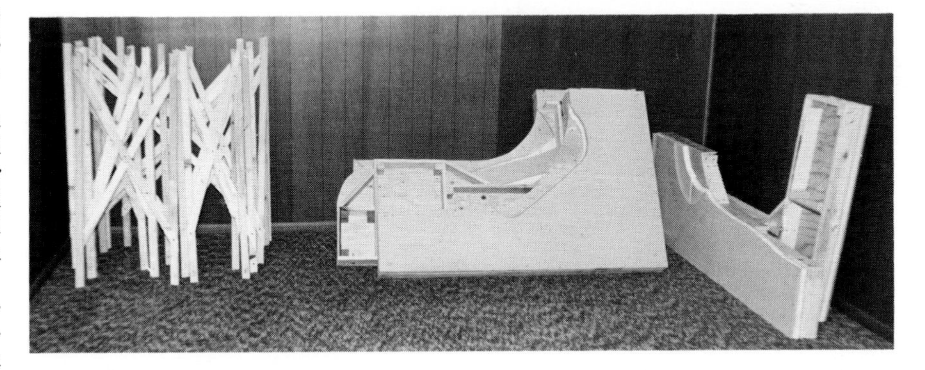

FIG. 10. THE COMPLETED BENCHWORK
Above: Even without the skyboards the benchwork makes a surprisingly small pile when disassembled. **Below:** Here's the mini-BN being put back together in Ed's basement.

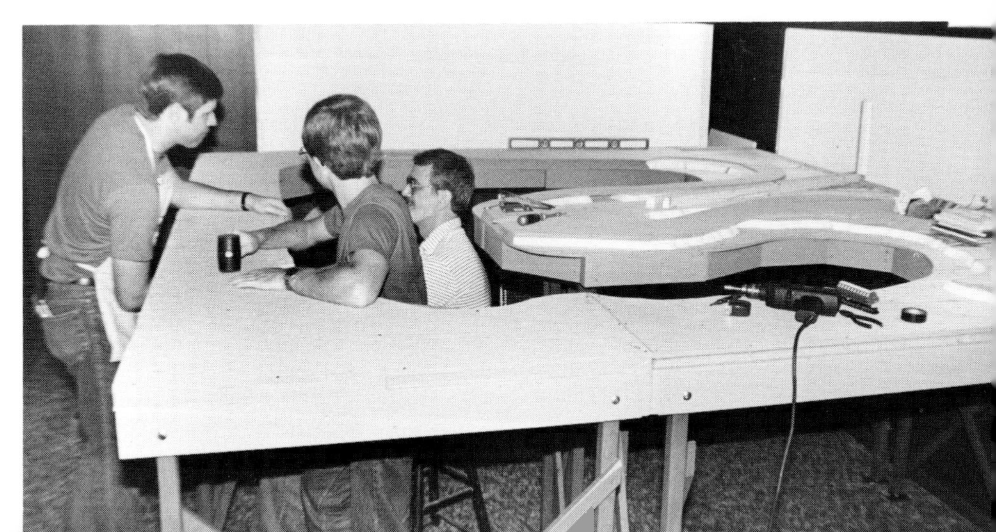

A. L. Schmidt

Laying track and building hills on the Burlington Northern

Our lightweight hills are made from Styrofoam insulation panels

BY ED HAMMER
PHOTOS BY THE BN BUILDERS

LAST MONTH we discussed building the benchwork for our N scale Burlington Northern. Once it was finished we attached five screw-on power strips, and these became very handy for plugging in power tools. This month we'll add cork roadbed, rough in some scenery with sheet Styrofoam, and then lay the track.

LAYING CORK ROADBED

Last time we mentioned we were using computer-drawn templates to mark the layout edges and riverbanks. Using these same templates it was a simple matter to mark the track center lines on the Homasote by poking through with a sharp instrument, as shown in fig. 1. We marked long stretches of straight track every few feet, curves every ½" or so, being careful to use about a ⅛" easement where the curve joined the straight (tangent) section. These gentle transitions make trains look better entering curves and a lot less likely to derail.

We connected the dots on the curves by freehand, although you really don't need to. As you lay the cork roadbed it will "find" the proper curvature.

For the straight stretches we connected the dots with a metal straightedge. Figure 2 shows how we laid the

Burlington Northern 3125, a Kato GP50, takes sustenance at the small service terminal just north of Prairie du Chien. In the background is the colossal 3M plant, largest employer in town. We think that one open door is a nice touch.

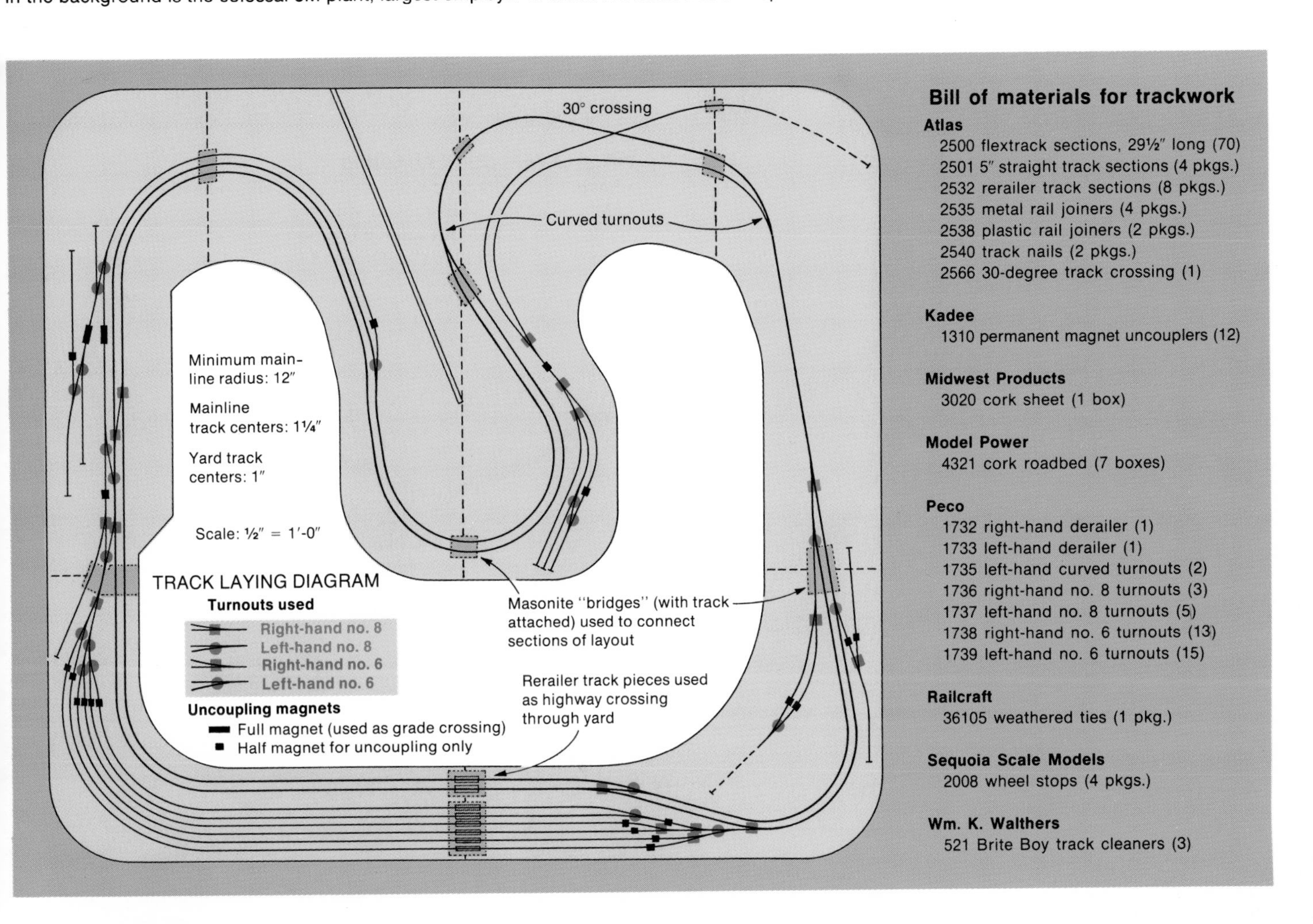

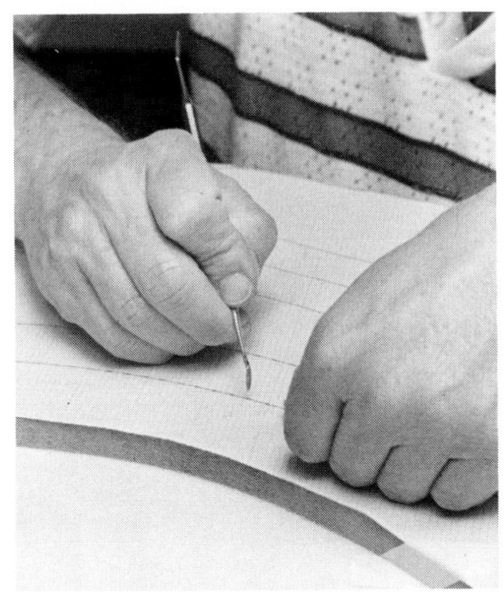

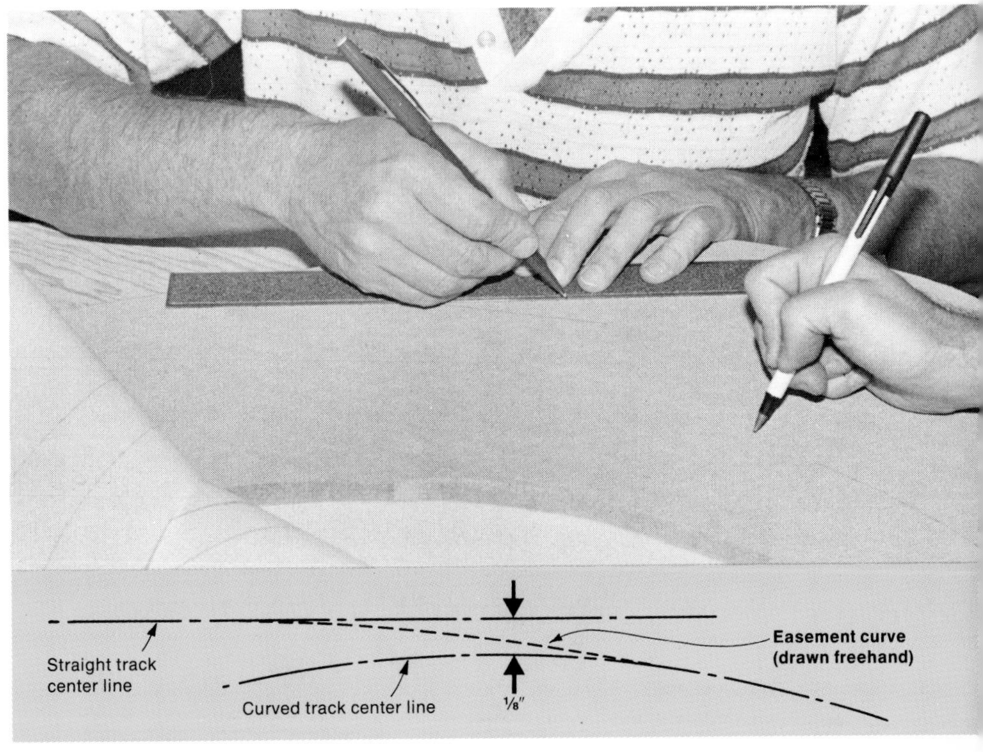

FIG. 1. MARKING TRACK CENTERS
Above: Any pointed instrument (here a dental probe) will do for poking holes in the paper template to mark the track center lines. **Above right:** Curves were marked by connecting the dots freehand. Straight sections were marked using a straightedge.

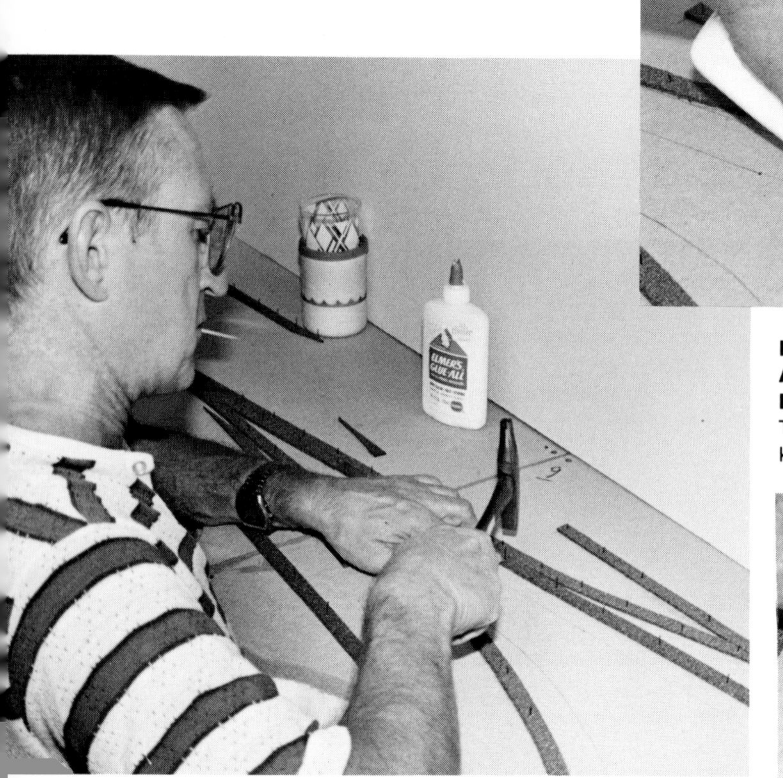

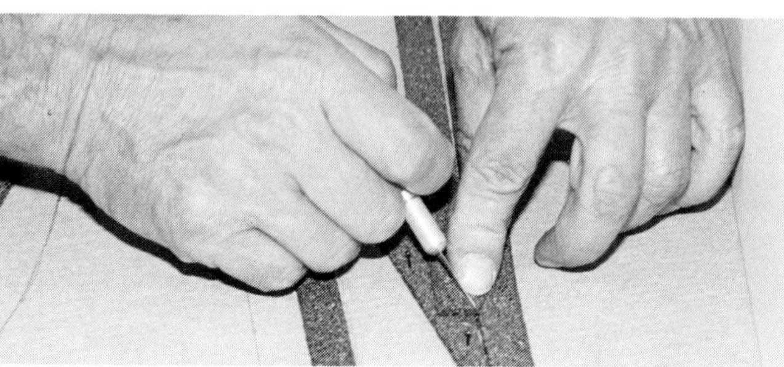

FIG. 2. LAYING CORK ROADBED
Above: Each cork strip half was secured with a bead of white glue. **Left:** The strips were tacked with track nails driven in halfway. These were pulled out after the glue had dried. **Below:** A hobby knife with a no. 11 blade was used to trim roadbed for the turnouts.

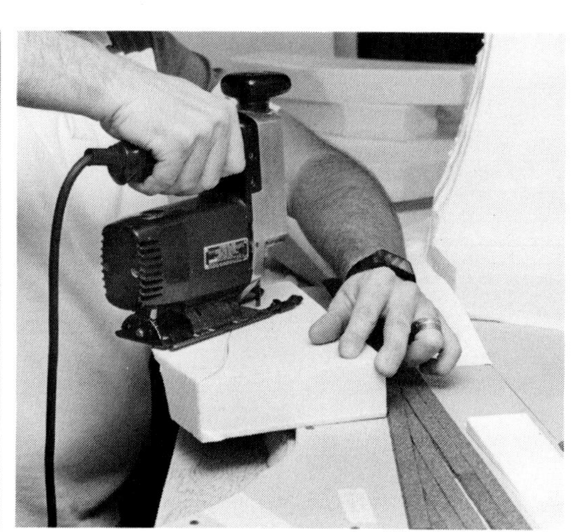

FIG. 3. FOAM SCENERY
Left: Here's a hill built up with layers of Styrofoam insulation. **Lower left:** The same hill, seen from a slightly different angle, has been carved to final shape, using a variety of cutting tools. **Above:** A saber saw works well for cutting the initial contours. **Below:** Here a keyhole saw is being used for shaping. Just about any kind of saw or knife works well.

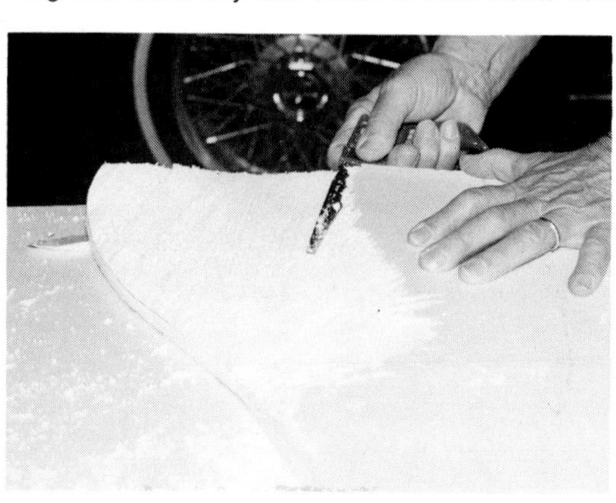

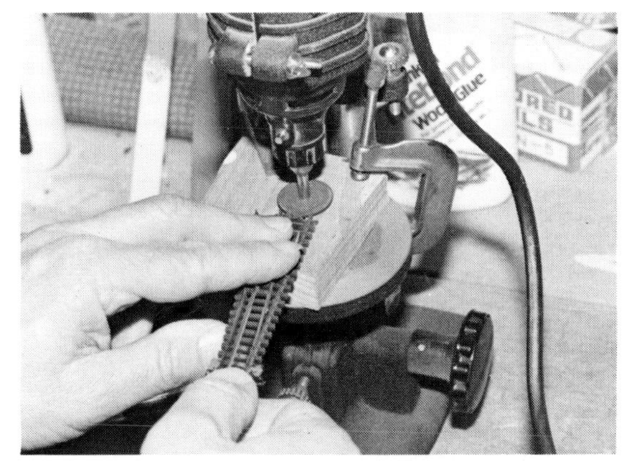

FIG. 4. TURNOUT MODIFICATIONS
Upper left: The flangeways on the Peco turnouts were narrowed by attaching styrene strips to the guardrails. **Lower left:** The strips were bonded with CA. **Lower right:** A chisel blade was used to trim strips. **Upper right:** The cast spikes on the first tie at each end of the turnout are removed, using a cutoff disk in a motor tool.

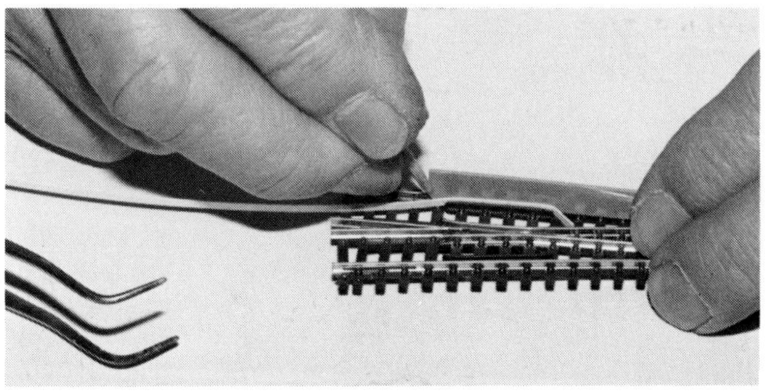

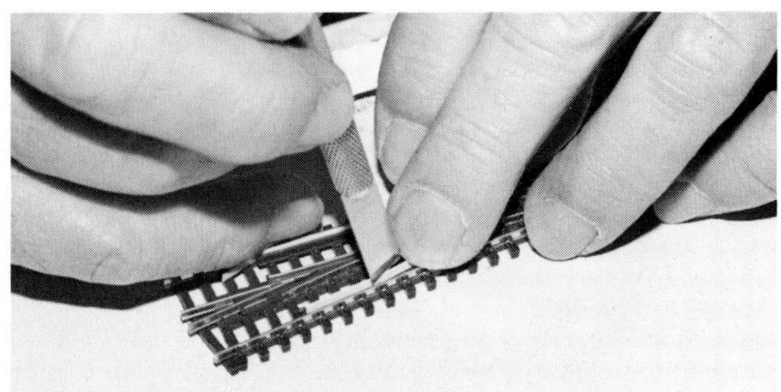

cork with white glue, holding it in position with Atlas track nails. The nails were shoved only partially in and pulled out at the next work session.

Most of the cork we used was the typical beveled cork roadbed, in this instance from Model Power. However, we also used Midwest Products cork sheet for the main yard between Prairie du Chien and Cassville and for the industrial sidings in Prairie. Prior to laying any cork roadbed, we rounded the outside corners with a 1-inch belt sander.

One tip: It's easier to lay the cork for a turnout if you do the two outside segments first. Then you can cut and fit the cork that goes to the inside.

At this stage it's hard to restrain folks from laying the track so they can see the trains run. That's only natural, and maybe that's the way you'll do it on your mini-BN. On ours we decided to rough in the bluffs first so we wouldn't have to cover the tracks or worry about getting glue on them. Nor would we have to dig our arms, elbows, and knees into the rails while climbing onto the layout in the Crawford Junction area.

THE BASIC LANDFORMS

The bluffs were made from 1″ and 2″ sheet Styrofoam. See fig. 3. This material comes in 4 x 8-foot sheets and is available in a variety of thicknesses. You may want to check your local building supply store to see what they carry and what would be most economical, as it doesn't matter what thickness you use. Also, you might ask to go through the scrap piles at local home building sites — I've found good-sized, 1″-thick pieces this way.

One of the more perplexing questions was how high to make the backdrop bluffs. The real ones range from 300 to 400 feet, but 300-foot bluffs in N scale would come out about 22″ high, leaving only 2″ of sky on our skyboards.

We mocked up an 18″ bluff and placed an engine and four or five cars on the cork roadbed in front of it. To say the result was overpowering would be putting it mildly. Finally we settled on a bluff height in the 13″ to 14″ range, rising to 17″ at the tip of the peninsula. Seeing trains in this latter area gives you the feeling that even as large as trains are, they're still a small part of the total environment.

Most of the scenery was built up with horizontal layers of foam, but as you can see in the photos, vertical slabs also worked out well in a place or two. We used a variety of tools to shape the Styrofoam. Those that worked best were the Stanley Surfoam shaver tools in differing shapes, an old table knife honed to a sharp edge, and the usual assortment of hobby knives. In looking at the photos you'll note that small, odd-shaped pieces of Styrofoam were glued to the near-vertical faces along the back skyboard in an attempt to break up the flatness of the bluffs.

The no. 5 hobby knife with X-acto's no. 226 whittling blade did yeoman's duty throughout the project. There wasn't much it could not accomplish. Of course some people never learn! One evening Jack Hillebrandt tried to cut off his thumb with the old no. 226, and we had to rush him to the emergency room. Fortunately it took only four stitches to close up the wound.

Blue hills are a little jarring to the eyeballs, even in a layout's early stages, so we finished our scenery forms by painting them with tan latex paint. Unwanted dips and hollows were filled in with Sculptamold, and we also used this material to smooth our riverbanks.

PREPPING THE TURNOUTS

Turnouts are the trickiest part of trackwork and difficult to work on once installed, so we performed some preparatory work on them at the workbench. Our experience has shown that even properly gauged Kadee wheelsets sometimes pick a switch point and derail at the frog of a Peco turnout. To eliminate this problem we narrowed the flangeways by cementing Evergreen .010″ x .080″ styrene strips to the guardrails, as shown in fig. 4.

Next we taped the turnout points where they contact the rail and attached the rail joiners to all six rail ends. Then we spray-painted the turnouts Rail Brown.

We also ballasted the turnouts before

FIG. 5. BALLASTING TURNOUTS
Above: Turnouts were ballasted before laying to avoid gluing them shut. Step one was placing electrical tape on the backs. **Right:** Ballast was poured on the turnout and pressed into place; then excess was dumped.

installing them so as to avoid gluing the points shut later. Figure 5 shows show we accomplished this by applying electrical tape to the bottoms of the ties. Then we sprinkled on the ballast. (In a later article we'll go into the colors used on various parts of the layout. For now, a medium gray is fine, as this ballast will be supplemented later — except around the points.) To finish the job we turned the turnout over and dumped the excess ballast back into the ballast container.

LAYING TRACK

The first step in laying track was placing the turnouts in their proper locations. On turnout ladders we carefully aligned the through straight rail with a steel straightedge, as shown in fig. 6. Now is a good time to point out that we cut off a single tie from the end of the flextrack where it was to be joined to the adjacent track with a rail joiner.

In the curves we let the track flex naturally rather than forcing it to follow any kinks we might have introduced in drawing the center line. On the straight sections we used both a 4-foot-long aluminum straightedge *and* the ol' eyeball to achieve straight lines.

We fastened the track down with Atlas track nails, *except* for the turnouts, which we allowed to float wherever possible. You may need nails to position the turnouts, but they can be pulled out later, as it is our judgment that the adjacent rail joiners will do a very satisfactory job of holding the turnouts in place. The primary reason for letting turnouts float is to reduce stress and warping in them.

A side benefit of this floating turnout technique is that later you can easily replace a turnout if the need arises. Just slide the rail joiners off the joints and lift the turnout out. In those areas where we had turnouts back to back, we violated the floating rule by using one track nail near the joint between the two turnouts. These track nails help to ensure correct alignment and can easily be removed after ballasting.

A word to the wise about using track nails — driving them too deep may distort the ties and pull the two rails closer together, thus narrowing the track gauge. Be careful to avoid doing this. Even if your rolling stock doesn't derail, you may have introduced extra wheel friction that the locomotives will have to overcome.

If you're going to leave in the track nails, you should check the gauge on the entire layout before ballasting. For better appearance, though, I recommend pulling the nails after you ballast the track, a subject we'll cover a few months from now. The glue used with the ballast will hold the track nicely.

For those locations where we knew we would need an insulated rail joint, we used Atlas plastic rail joiners. For those blocks determined later, we used the razor saw or rotary tool with the regular-duty cutoff wheel to cut both rails. Then we used cyanoacrylate adhesive (CA) to cement thin strips of styrene into the gaps to help maintain the correct gauge. This also prevents the gap from closing should the rails expand from temperature and humidity variations. After the CA had dried, we shaped the styrene with small files to blend it in with the rail.

Meanwhile, back at the rail joiners. We soldered as many of them as possible while laying the track to ensure that the rails wouldn't slide. Also, where we knew a joint would fall on a curve we first soldered two straight sections together, then carefully bent them, starting from the joint, and installed them. This helps achieve a smoother transition than trying to solder the joint in place on the curve.

The main exception to our "solder-all-the-joints" rule was any rail joiner on a turnout. You may want to make additional exceptions if the layout will be subject to temperature or humidity changes. It's conceivable that the rails could expand and kinks be introduced. A few unsoldered joints with slight gaps would alleviate this problem.

Also, you don't want to solder those rail joiners located at either end of the Masonite bridges crossing a table joint. These should be removable so you can disassemble the layout and reassemble it elsewhere, as we did for Milwaukee's Trainfest '89 a few months ago.

THE MASONITE BRIDGES

"Whoa!" you say. "What's with the Masonite bridges you just mentioned?"

Well, we needed some way to bridge the gap between layout sections easily, and these were our solution. Many of today's modular railroading systems — Ntrak, for one — use standard lengths of sectional straight track to bridge the gaps between modules. This ensures correct alignment and a good, tight fit of track that helps the operators by providing a convenient method of setting up and tearing down for a train show.

We didn't have standard interfaces, though, and some of our connecting tracks were curved, so we devised a slightly different method of accomplishing the same thing. See fig. 7.

Once all the track was laid, we used masking tape to mark where the Masonite bridges would go, making sure that all turnouts remained intact. Then with a razor saw we carefully cut the tracks along the masking tape.

Next we cut a piece of ⅛" Masonite to fit the area. The Masonite is slightly thicker than the cork roadbed, so we had to chisel and carve away some Homasote. The critical areas were those adjacent to the connecting tracks. Other areas could be excavated somewhat deeper; thus the term "Masonite bridge" was coined.

FIG. 6. LAYING TRACK

Above: Turnout groups were assembled on the workbench, then laid as an assembly. **Top right:** A straightedge was used to check straight track. **Above right:** The same instrument turned on edge was good for checking curves. **Middle right:** Homemade gauges were a great help in keeping parallel tracks parallel. **Right:** This homemade tool kept rails in gauge while rail joints were soldered.

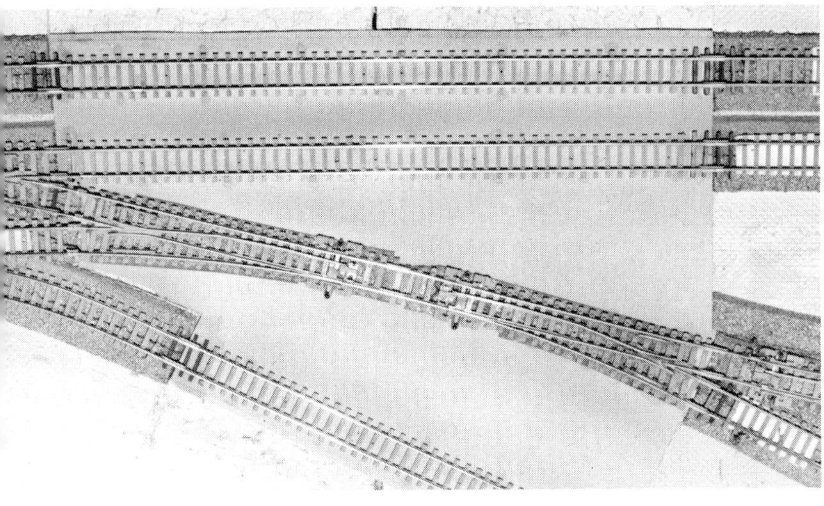

FIG. 7. MASONITE BRIDGES

Above: Tracks connecting layout sections were cemented to Masonite bridges like this one, making the layout easy to take down and put back together. **Above right:** First step in making these bridges was marking their limits with masking tape and cutting out the tracks. **Right:** Here's a Masonite bridge cut to fit, edges beveled. The Homasote will be relieved enough to make the top of the Masonite come out even with the top of the roadbed.

A Kato GP50, Interrail double-stack car in tow, crossing the Wisconsin River where it flows into the Mississippi.

FIG. 8. RERAILER ROADWAY
Above: Atlas rerailers were used on the Masonite bridge connecting the two halves of the staging yard. **Below:** The modelers used a band saw to cut the rerailer edges off square so pieces of roadbed cork could be inserted in between to form a road.

FIG. 9. UNCOUPLER MAGNETS
Ties were removed with a cutoff disk in a motor tool. Before being installed, the Kadee magnets were scribed and broken in half.

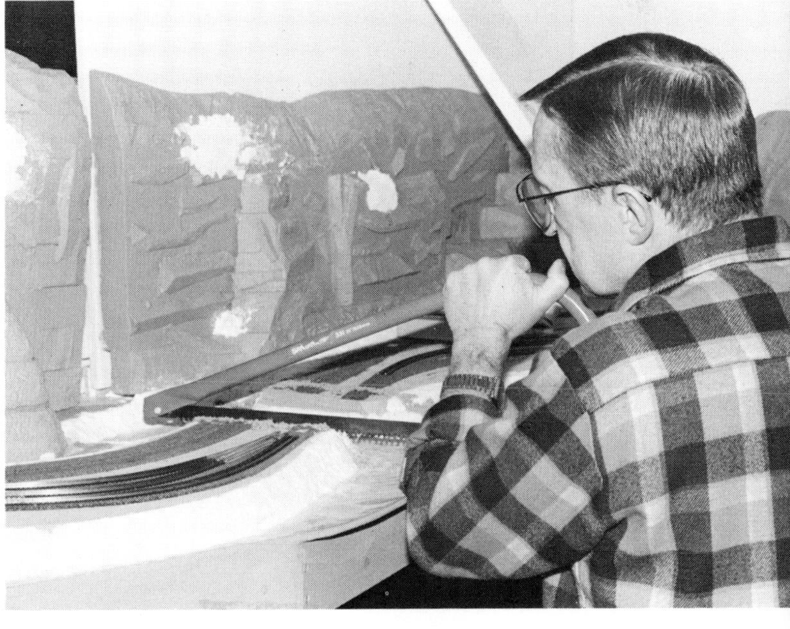

FIG. 10. BRIDGE ABUTMENTS
Above: The first step in installing bridges was cutting through the Homasote/foam sandwich. Our author took plenty of tool for the job! **Top left:** Here's the roadbed ready for the abutments to be added. **Left:** Concrete retaining walls were represented with Masonite blocks. **Below left:** The concrete walls were finished off with wood putty. Simple concrete deck bridges were represented with Masonite and stripwood. **Below:** Stepped abutments made of Masonite support this pair of Micro Engineering steel deck girder bridges.

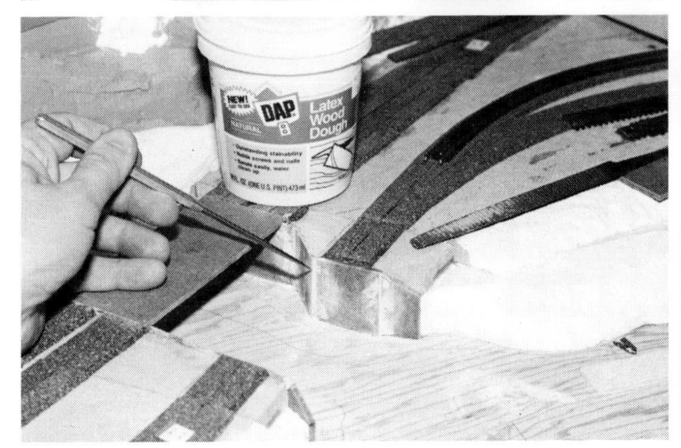

We beveled the edges of the Masonite bridges with a 1-inch belt sander so they would match the cork roadbed. After putting each bridge in place, we reinstalled the tracks. Once satisfied with the alignment, we secured the ties to the Masonite with CA.

"But," you ask, "what can I do if the area I'm working in has some curved flextrack?" No problem! Since the curve is already laid exactly as you want it, just use CA to lock the track and ties together before cutting the rails with the razor saw. Be careful not to cement the ties to the Homasote. Remove the track, and it will hold its curve perfectly.

For the Masonite bridge crossing the middle of the main yard, we replaced the track removed with Atlas rerailers to represent a highway crossing. As shown in fig. 8, we trimmed off the plastic edges flush with the ties, using a 10″ band saw. After fastening down the rerailers with CA, we cemented strips of cork roadbed between them to complete the crossing.

Cutting, fitting, and trimming those Masonite bridges isn't difficult, but it does take a little time. Don't rush it, and for that matter, don't rush through any of the trackwork. Skimp, if you must, elsewhere on this project, but don't even consider skimping on the time needed to lay the track well. Your reward will be much better operation!

UNCOUPLING RAMPS AND BRIDGES

We used Kadee no. 1310 permanent magnet uncouplers, carefully breaking them in half to get two uncouplers for the price of one. To install them we first cut the ties between the rails as shown in fig. 9, using a motor tool with a cutoff disc. Also, we used full-length uncouplers in a couple of locations where the magnet could double as a roadway crossing. The magnets were fastened down with Walthers Goo.

Beats there a heart so cold that it doesn't warm to the sight of a train crossing a bridge? Most of ours were made from Micro Engineering kits. We also used several simple concrete deck bridges supported on concrete piles made from 3/16″ Plastruct tubing. Figure 10 shows how we made abutments.

But bridges are structures, folks, so maybe we've gotten a step ahead of ourselves. For structures, you see, is the subject for next month. See you then!

PRAIRIE
DU CHIEN

Running short and hot, a Burli
town Prairie du Chien, Wis. The a
railroad built for MODEL RAILROAD
modelers and introduced in ou
the layout's structures. One of
Tavern, just across the tracks he

Structures for our N scale Burlington Northern

How about adding some of these to your own pike?

BY ED HAMMER

PHOTOS BY THE BN BUILDERS

LAST MONTH, we laid the track and installed the Styrofoam landforms for our N scale Burlington Northern. This month we'll discuss structures. Counting bridges and shacks, there are 55 of them, so I can't get into a lot of nitty-gritty on each and every one. Rather, I'll cover some of the basic materials and techniques, then show some of the more unusual or interesting buildings in separate boxes, along with notes on how to build them. Most of you aren't going to build our mini-BN, but here's hoping there's a structure or two in this lot that will find a home on your layout.

Figure 1 shows where each structure is located and includes

A. L. Schmidt

Jorthern train sweeps into down-
akes place on a 9 x 10-foot N scale
azine by a group of Madison, Wis.,
ary issue. This month we'll cover
orites is Jack Hillebrandt's Ziel's
d to believe, but this is a kitbash!

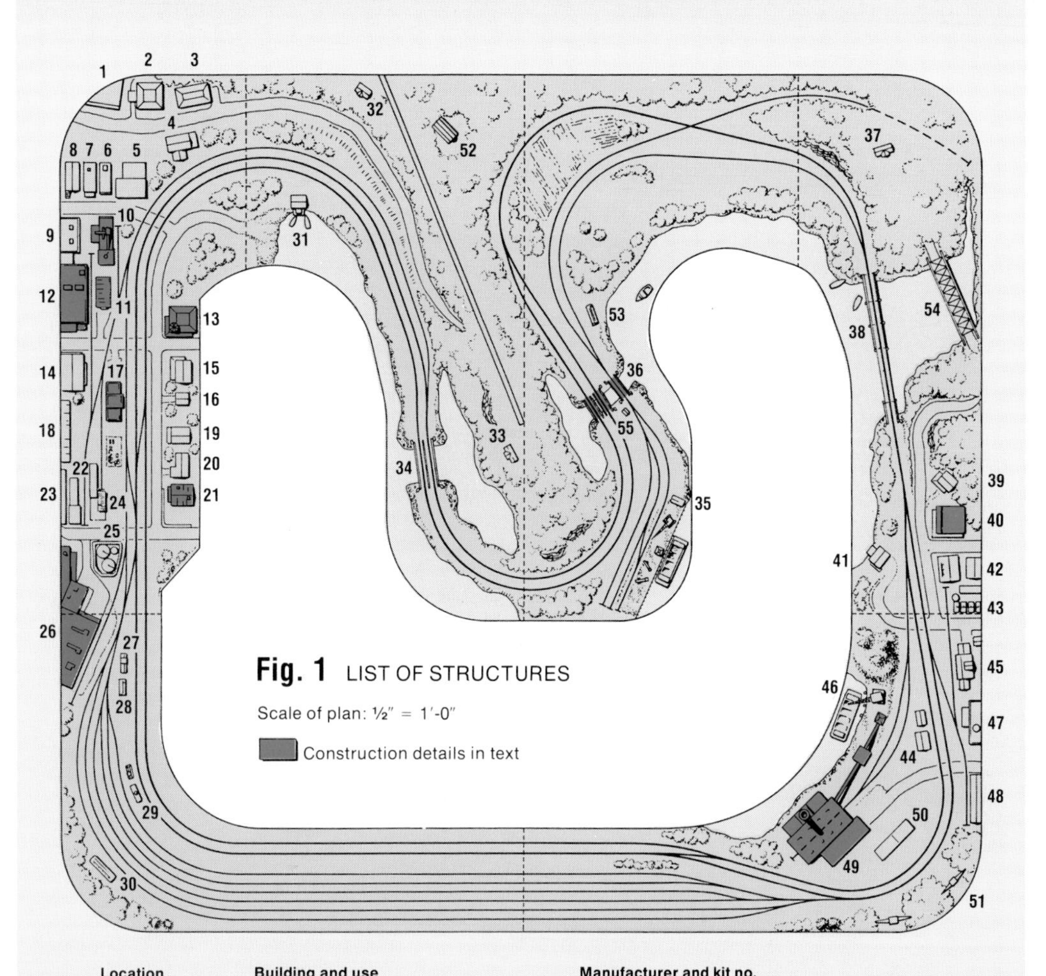

Location		Building and use	Manufacturer and kit no.
1	B	Storefront	Heljan no. 609 Lyric Theater
2	B	Burger King	LL no. 7462 Burger King
3	K	Pizza Hut	LL no. 7467 Pizza Hut
4	K	House	Bachmann no. 7312 Farmhouse
5	S	Valley Feed Lot (office)	H&R brick siding, PM doors and windows
6	K	Storefront	IHC no. 20016 Rita's Antique Shop
7	K	House	IHC no. 2004 Painted Lady Gingerbread
8	K	Ice cream parlor	Heljan (also IHC) no. 604 Woolworth's Store
9	K	Woolworth's	Heljan no. 604 Woolworth's Store
10	S	Valley Feed Mill	See description
11	K	Quonset garage	See description
12	B	Doc Thompson's plant	See description
13	B	Ziel's Tavern	See description
14	B	Doc Thompson's offices	ME no. 55003 Petroff Plumbing
15	K	House	LL no. 7432 Farmhouse
16	S	Garage/shed	GC no. 224 Section House
17	S	CB&Q passenger station	See description
18	F	General office (flat)	ME no. 55001 Murphy Manufacturing Co.
19	B	House	LL no. 7432 Farmhouse
20	K	House	LL no. 7414 Farmhouse
21	B	*Zephyr* Bar	See description
22	K	Prairie du Chien Lumberyard	GC no. 201 Cash & Carry Lumber
23	B	Warehouse (flat)	Heljan no. 672 Furniture Factory
24	B	Storage shed	TP Products no. 210 Gordon White Furniture Co.
25	B	3M storage tanks	Campbell 18-foot Storage Tanks
26	B	3M plant	ME no. 55002 Truck Terminal
27	K	Engine crew shed	Alloy Forms no. 128
28	K	Yardmaster's office	Alloy Forms no. 129
29	K	Diesel oil storage tank	Stewart no. 1107
30	K	Track gang baggage house	Chooch no. 9805
31	K	Prairie du Chien boat landing	PM no. 204 Mel's Produce
32	K	House (Z scale)	Kibri no. 6780
33	K	House (Z scale)	Kibri no. 6782
34	K	Deck plate girder bridges	ME no. 150 (2)
35	K	Office shack	CS Models no. 101 Lineside Buildings
36	S	Concrete deck bridges	See description
37	K	House (Z scale)	Kibri no. 6780
38	K	Deck plate girder bridge (240 feet)	ME nos. 150, 151 bridges
39	K	House	Bachmann no. 7312 Farmhouse
40	B	Denniston House hotel	See description
41	K	Riverfront home	PM no. 204 Mel's Produce
42	K	Kadee Lumber Co.	GC no. 201 Lumber Company
43	K	Adrian Oil Co.	Kibri no. 2456 Storage Tanks
44	S	BN offices	Northeastern wood siding
45	K	Cassville Feed Mill	Heljan no. 670 Grain Mill
46	K	Coal barge unloader	Faller no. 2190 Gantry Crane
47	B	Warehouse (flat)	Heljan no. 672 Furniture Factory
48	B	Small industry	ME no. 55001 Murphy Manufacturing Co.
49	S	Nelson Dewey Power Plant	See description
50	K	Electric substation	Green Max no. 25 (2)
51	K	High line towers	Brawa no. 2658
52	B	Barn	Kibri no. 6782
53	K	Section house	GC no. 224
54	K	Highway 18 bridge	Arnold no. 6170
55	K	Scale shed	Stewart no. 1107

ABBREVIATIONS

B = Kitbashed
K = Kit-built straight out of the box
S = Scratchbuilt

ME = Micro Engineering
GC = Gloor Craft
IHC = International Hobby Corp.
LL = Life-Like
PM = Period Miniatures

Both photos by A. L. Schmidt

FIG. 2. BAND SAW BASHING
Above: A band saw can be a wonderful modeling tool. In this Prairie du Chien scene the nondescript structure behind the lumberyard was sliced off a completed Heljan furniture factory. **Below:** The other side of the building, sporting yellow paint, was used in Cassville.

basic information on whether it was built straight from a box, kitbashed, or scratchbuilt. In several cases, the kitbashing amounted to nothing more than running a completed building through a 10″ band saw to cut it down to size, as shown in fig. 2.

ADHESIVES

We used the following glues to assemble the structures:

• Liquid plastic cement was the principal adhesive for the styrene structures.

• CA (cyanoacrylate adhesive, also called super glue) was used on some of the plastic and some of the wooden structures. We used both Instant Jet (sets in about 15 seconds) and Super Jet (sets in about 15-20 seconds and has gap-filling qualities). Zap-A-Gap, as the name implies, is another CA with a gap-filling formula. We used it extensively for scratchbuilding.

To use one of the instant glues on wood structures, we first applied a coat of CA to the surfaces to be bonded so that it would absorb into the wood and dry. Then we used a second coat to bind the wood pieces together.

• Good old white glue was used for several of the wooden structures.

• Walthers Goo, applied extensively, was used to mount structures directly onto the tabletop. A word of caution, however — Goo will attack Styrofoam, as we learned with some of our buildings that had foam bases. Even a coat of latex paint won't protect the Styrofoam. We also used Goo to secure the details added to the layout in its final stages.

BASIC APPROACHES

Many N scale structure kits are available today, ranging from "shake-the-box" plastic kits to some excellent craftsman-type wood kits.

The Bachmann structures and Brawa electric transmission towers we used on

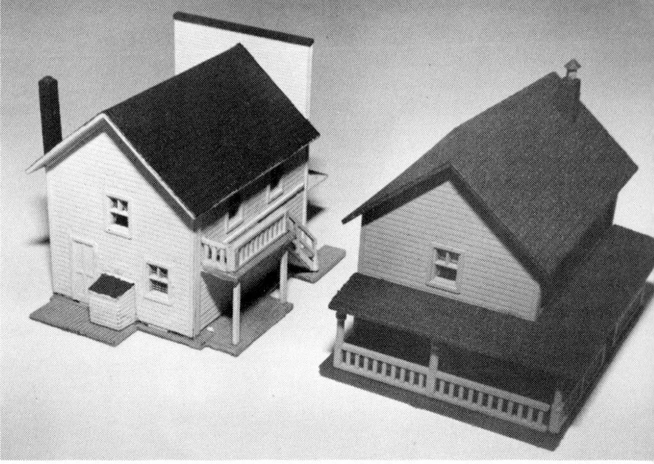

FIG. 3. TWO KITBASHED HOUSES

There's more to a kit than meets the eye. It's hard to believe, but these two structures were made from identical kits, Life-Like no. 7432 farmhouses. The false-front building (no. 19 in fig. 1) has an Evergreen scribed styrene front with Grandt Line windows added. The other house (no. 15) is stock except the lean-to was left off.

VALLEY FEED MILL (10)

George Nelson built this one for us. Most towns in the rural Midwest have similar structures, as there are a lot of mouths to feed out there, and most of them are on cows, pigs, and chickens.

Here the idea was not to build an exact duplicate, but rather a building that looked similar and would work. Grains and other feed ingredients can be stored in various parts of the building, ground to various grades, moved about and combined, and delivered (bulk or bagged) to the customer.

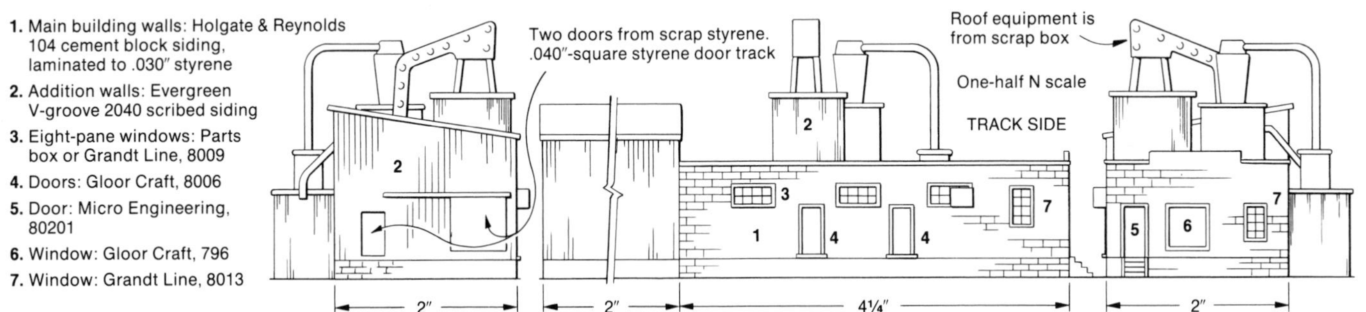

the layout came preassembled and ready to use. All we did with the Bachmann buildings was add some paint or Testor's Dullcote in an attempt to conceal their heritage and tone down their shininess. We've found in practically all cases that plastic kits are unnaturally colored and glossy and need painting.

The Model Power and Life-Like structures practically fall together as the pieces are dumped from the box, so start with those if you're just getting started in kit building. These are very interesting beginner kits, but it probably wouldn't take too many of them before you'd like a bigger challenge.

One way to enhance these kits is to add lots of details — they are barren of much of the clutter and junk that give a home or business that lived-in look. Adding a chimney or two usually won't hurt either. Such kits are also excellent for a first kitbashing project. See fig. 3.

The remainder of the plastic kits — Heljan, Arnold, IHC, Micro Engineering, TP Products, Kibri, and Green Max — are a little more advanced, but don't let that intimidate you. Like the Life-Like and Model Power kits, these are excellent. With some ingenuity and imagination, you can kitbash them into a host of different structures.

Looking at fig. 1, perhaps you've noticed that several of our major facilities had their origins in Micro Engineering kits. I assure you we weren't out to build a tribute to Micro Engineering, though it may seem like it. Things worked out that way because their modern metal

PRAIRIE DU CHIEN STATION (17)

George Nelson built this gem. This is one of the few buildings we measured, even getting the height with the use of a stadia rod. He used Holgate & Reynolds no. 1011 brick siding laminated to .030" styrene for the exterior walls. The windows and doors are by Period Miniatures and Model Power. The exterior lights are by Gloor Craft, while the loading dock is Micro Engineering's. The tall antenna is an Atlas HO telephone pole, and the telephone box is by Wheel Works. The roof and the horizontal strips are of sheet styrene.

Using an airbrush George painted the brick walls with a 1:1 mixture of Floquil Boxcar Red and Roof Brown, while the trim is Roof Brown. The roof is Black oversprayed with Dust, and the horizontal strips encircling the structure are Concrete. The exterior walls were weathered by dry-brushing them with both Black and SP Armour Yellow.

DOC THOMPSON'S PLANT (12)

Marc Van Cleven kitbashed the A. W. Thompson plant from one Micro Engineering Murphy Manufacturing kit, some leftover parts from the 3M plant, Plastruct channels, and Evergreen styrene sheets and strips. The prototype plant manufactures minerals and premixes for livestock feed.

What makes Doc Thompson's especially interesting is the cast-concrete foundation with sheet-metal doors placed in various spots along the side. The roof border trim along the entire building is also distinctive.

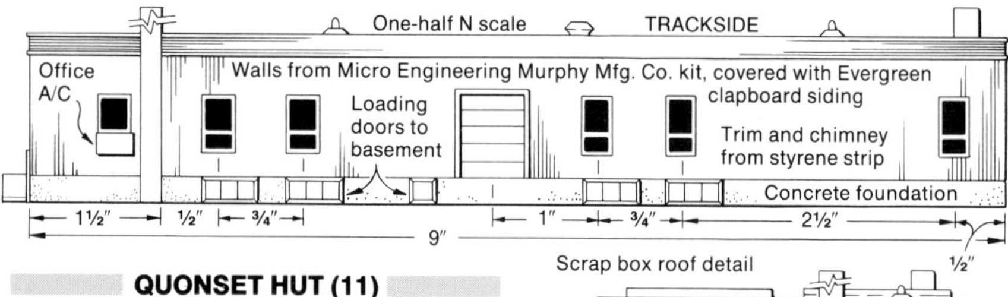

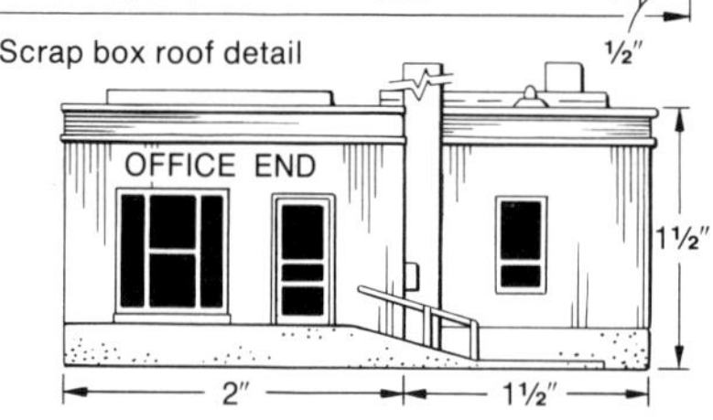

QUONSET HUT (11)

Ed Hammer built the quonset hut, which is used by a wrecker service. He started with half of a Williams no. 501 HO vertical storage tank. The ends are half-circles cut from sheet styrene.

The building is covered with Williams no. 600 HO corrugated aluminum. Ed coated both surfaces to be joined with Sanford's rubber cement, let it dry for a few minutes, then "rolled" the siding on.

ZIEL'S OLD FAITHFUL INN (13)

This is one of two taverns located across the street from the old passenger station in Prairie du Chien. Jack Hillebrandt, our "master builder," kitbashed this beautiful structure.

The window frames, corner, and two sides all come from a Heljan no. 601 Two Bros.

ZEPHYR BAR (21)

This is another of Jack Hillebrandt's beauties. He kitbashed it from a Life-Like

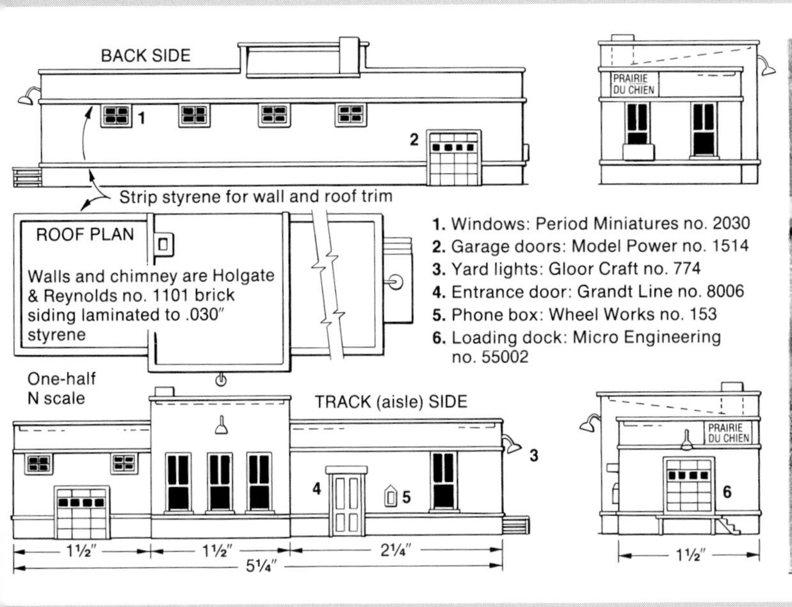

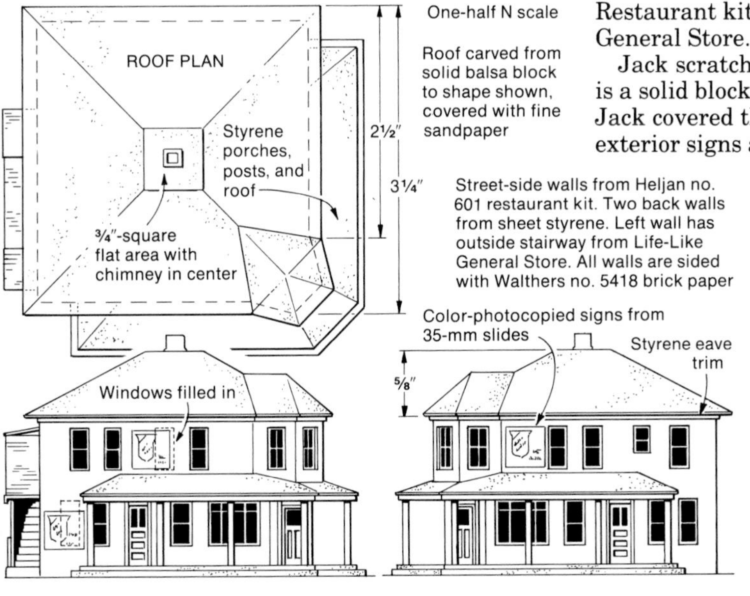

Restaurant kit. The stairway on the left side is from Life-Like's no. 7406 General Store.

Jack scratchbuilt the rest of the building from sheet styrene. The roof is a solid block of balsa wood, with sandpaper added to represent roofing. Jack covered the styrene walls with Walthers no. 5418 brick paper. The exterior signs are from color photos, reduced to size on a color copier.

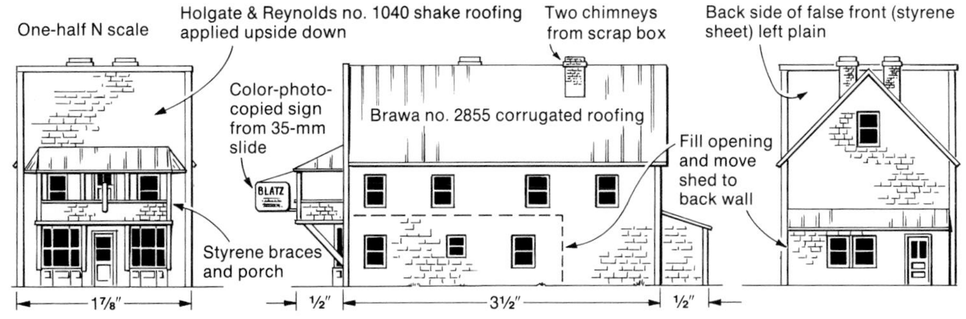

no. 7406 General Store kit. The front balcony and rear porch are scratchbuilt.

Jack applied Holgate & Reynolds no. 1011 brick upside down to simulate the "cut stone" the prototype metal siding tries to emulate. He made signs on a color copier from prototype photos; the main one has *Zephyr* Bar on one side, Florence Hill on the other.

3M PLANT (26)

Marc Van Cleven outdid himself on this one. The actual complex is very large, encompassing many acres, and was impossible to model in its entirety, given our space limitations. Part of the solution was to angle the building, suggesting that half or more of it lies beyond the backdrop.

This complex sits astride a table joint, so we cemented it to a Masonite base that simply lifts off the layout. The buildings themselves have Fome-Cor bases that were cemented to the Masonite with Goo.

One-quarter N scale

Tall main building is sided with Evergreen corrugated-metal (styrene) building sheet (no. 4525)

Warehouse wings on either side are from Micro Engineering Trans World Truck Terminal kit (no. 55002)

Three large tanks at front of building (not shown) are Campbell HO horizontal storage tanks (no. 407)

Miscellaneous parts: Green Max Chemical Plant accessory kit

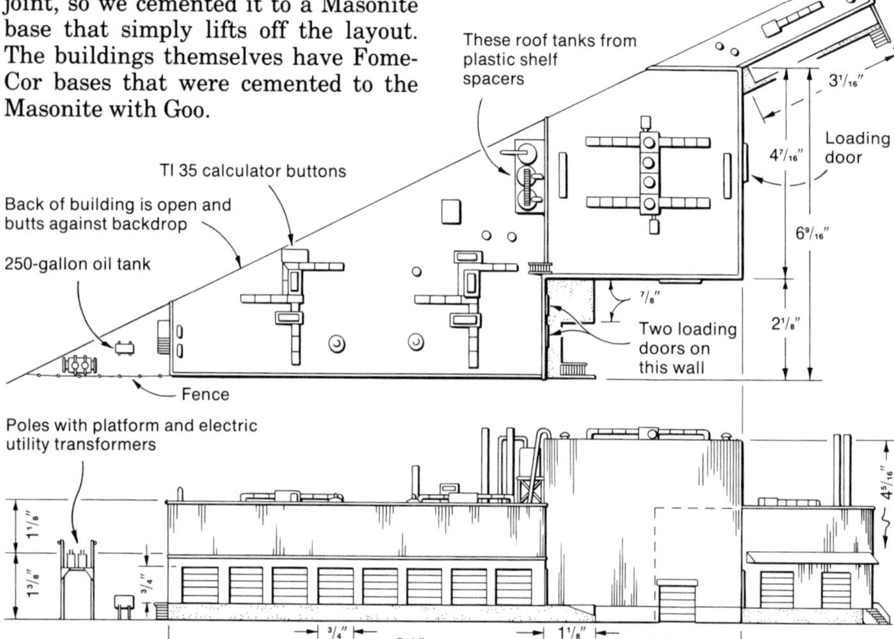

NELSON DEWEY POWER PLANT (49)

Like the 3M plant, this is a structure that was far too large to model actual size. And talk about your selective compression! The prototype stack stands 353 feet above the plant roadway. To match that we would have needed a 26½″ stack, but we settled for 17½″.

George Nelson built our compressed version, using Evergreen's styrene corrugated siding for all the walls and plain sheet styrene for the roofs. The vents on the main building roof are leftovers from the Green Max power substations.

The power distribution area is made of two Green Max no. 25 power substations. These fine kits, if not carried by your favorite hobby shop, are distributed by Lee Durham of Mokei Imports, 6950 Kingsbury, St. Louis, MO 63130. The small power poles are also from Green Max.

George says the biggest challenge in building the complex was the conveyor-belt assembly from the coal stockpile area to the power plant. Ed Hammer suggested using some of the girders from Central Valley's no. 1902-5 bridge girder kit. End of challenge!

The fence around the complex is fiber-glass screen cemented with CA to common straight pins stuck into the Homasote tabletop.

The entire complex was painted with a mixture of 2 parts Floquil Platinum Mist and 1 part Southern Pacific Lettering Grey. That was followed by an overspray of Dust, Grime, and Earth.

Finally, two blinking red light-emitting diodes (LED) were added at the top of the stack. A Radio Shack LED flasher (no. 276-1705) and electrolytic capacitor (no. 272-956) were used.

We would like to offer a special thank you to Bob Newell of Wisconsin Power & Light Co. in Madison for furnishing us with general drawings of the generating station.

CONCRETE DECK GIRDER BRIDGES (36)

We used ⅛″ Masonite to scratchbuild the decks and abutments; the cutting was done with a small band saw. The piers are Plastruct ³/₁₆″ tubes. Water is two-part epoxy.

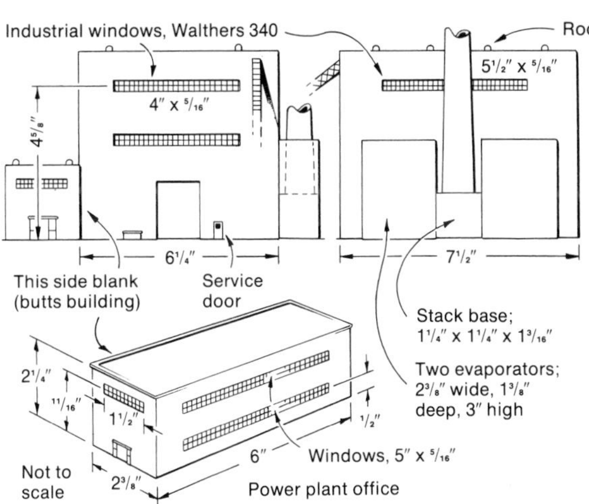

Industrial windows, Walthers 340
Roof vents, Green Max power substation parts
4″ x 5/16″
5 1/2″ x 5/16″
4 5/8″
6 1/4″
7 1/2″
This side blank (butts building)
Service door
Stack base; 1 1/4″ x 1 1/4″ x 1 3/16″
Two evaporators; 2 3/8″ wide, 1 3/8″ deep, 3″ high
2 1/4″
11/16″
1 1/2″
1/2″
6″
Windows, 5″ x 5/16″
Not to scale
2 3/8″
Power plant office

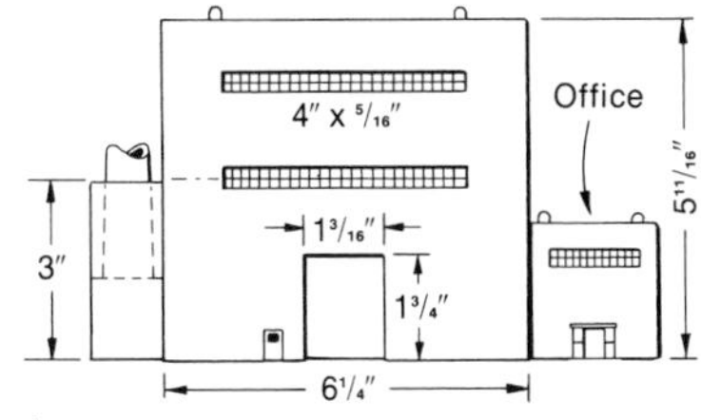

4″ x 5/16″
Office
5 11/16″
1 3/16″
3″
1 3/4″
6 1/4″

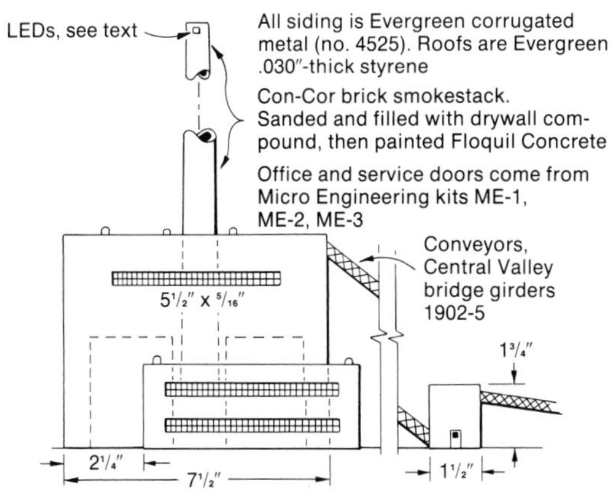

LEDs, see text
All siding is Evergreen corrugated metal (no. 4525). Roofs are Evergreen .030″-thick styrene
Con-Cor brick smokestack. Sanded and filled with drywall compound, then painted Floquil Concrete
Office and service doors come from Micro Engineering kits ME-1, ME-2, ME-3
Conveyors, Central Valley bridge girders 1902-5
5 1/2″ x 5/16″
1 3/4″
2 1/4″
7 1/2″
1 1/2″

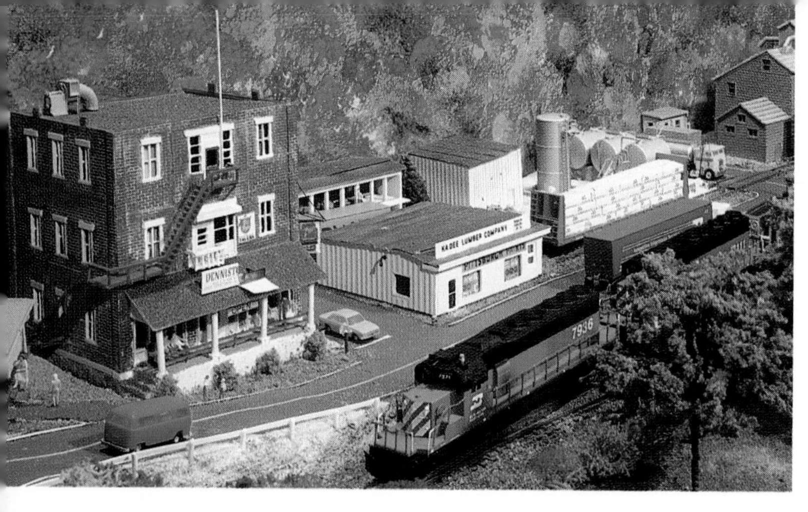

DENNISTON HOUSE (40)

This terrific little model was fashioned by Curt Hammer by combining two Model Power railroad hotel kits. The prototype is a historic landmark and has been operated continuously as a hotel since 1854.

Curt rubbed Ready Patch, a white spackling compound, into the three brick walls to simulate mortar. The back wall, which faces the skyboard, is simply a piece of plain painted styrene.

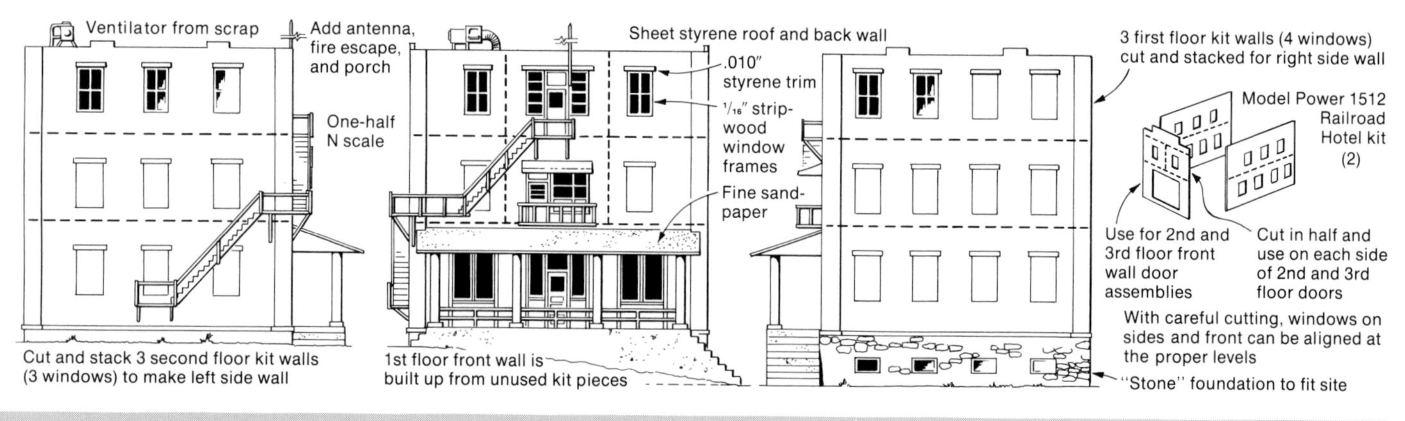

A. L. Schmidt

buildings are easy to kitbash and typical of what you see nowadays. We used lots of their deck girder bridges because they were dead ringers for our prototypes.

SOME FINAL THOUGHTS

Our structure builders made liberal use of their parts bins, so I recommend you set aside an old cigar box, shoe box, or whatever, and start a spare parts bin of your own. You'll be amazed at how rapidly it fills up and how often you'll find in it that perfect treasure to finish a project. Save all the leftover pieces from everything you put together; sooner or later you'll find uses for them.

I hope that you'll enjoy this brief architectural tour through our Mississippi River communities. Next month we'll wire the railroad. That ought to get your juices flowing!

Left: The arrangement and details are everything. Most of the structures shown here are easily recognizable N scale models built straight from the box. Add a street, some figures, and a few details, and they look as if they've always been together.

Sailing comes to a halt as this boater sits back and watches the Burlington Northern whir past him.

Wiring our project layout

This traditional two-cab system is hard to beat for small pikes

Both photos by A. L. Schmidt

BY LEE ZEIS

PHOTOS BY THE BN BUILDERS

WIRING IS EASY! No foolin'! My plan was to wire our N scale Burlington Northern over my nine-day Christmas holiday. Ed Hammer didn't believe it could be done, so with his help, along with assistance from George Nelson, Mike Vivion, Marc Van Cleven, and Curt Hammer, we showed him.

DESIGN PHILOSOPHY

In planning to wire a railroad you need to decide what features you want. Our BN modelers came up with this list of *must haves*:

- Multiple cabs.
- Multiple panels.
- Walkaround throttles.
- KISS method: Keep It Simple, Stupid.

We also made a list of *would likes*:

- Memory walkaround throttles
- Block on/off indicators on panel
- Control panels not to extend below framework, for ease of portability.
- Layout picture rather than schematic type of panel.

DECISIONS, DECISIONS

Gathering the materials prior to starting makes a project flow smoother, but before you can do so you have to decide what you'll use.

After consulting with the MODEL RAILROADER staff, we chose the American Switch & Signal Model UT-1 Universal Throttle from Electroplumbing, 1918 Parklane, McHenry, IL 60050. See fig. 1. Andy Sperandeo reviewed this throttle in the December 1987 MR.

Above left: This month we'll wire our N scale railroad, so here's a shot taken at the Cassville power plant. Get the connection? We introduced our 9 x 10-foot project layout in February. It's based on the Burlington Northern's route along the Mississippi River in southwest Wisconsin.

Left: Coal unloaded from barges and destined for Madison is an important source of revenue for the Wisconsin & Calumet, a short line interchanging with the BN at Crawford Junction, near Prairie du Chien. The layout's barges were scratchbuilt by Dennis Pehoski, a Milwaukee N scaler.

[After writing this article the Madison group twice experienced component failures in these throttles. If you use the UT-1, we urge you to install overload protection as described in Andy's review. — *Ed.*]

How many throttles? Certainly we needed two for the main line, but did we really need the memory walkaround for the WICT? No, but having it gave us a spare if a mainline throttle broke.

Next we needed to decide the number and location of the electrical blocks. On this layout, deciding how to handle the single-track main line was the major consideration. Given train lengths and the size of the layout, five mainline blocks seemed just right. The yard tracks are one block, using the power-routing feature of the Peco turnouts. The block boundaries and feeder wire locations are shown in fig. 1.

Designing the control panels came next. Remember the design criteria? "Must have" multiple panels, "would like" them not to extend below the frame. The framework is 3½" high, so 2½" was about maximum for the panel height. You can't get a "picture type" of panel in 2½", so we went schematic.

The small panel size almost dictates using light-emitting diodes (LEDs) for the block on/off lights. LEDs have lots of advantages, foremost among them that they almost never burn out! But placing control panels vertically on the framework leads to a problem. LEDs have a viewing angle of approximately 45 degrees. Standing close to the panel and looking down at the LED, you wouldn't be able to tell it was on!

Did we really need indicator lights anyway? Not really. Let the toggle switch's position indicate the block's condition: Left = left throttle, center = off, right = right throttle.

Choosing the type and size of wire was easy. First, *always* use stranded wire under the layout. For a layout this small, voltage drops would be minimal unless extremely small wire sizes were used — 22 gauge would be sufficient.

We decided to use connectors between modules because we knew the layout would be moved at least three times.

Should we use terminal strips? Absolutely. Everyone makes mistakes in wiring; terminal strips make them much easier to correct.

PANEL CONSTRUCTION

I enjoy making control panels. My best ones are made from clear Plexiglas. For my home layout, I painted the back of the Plexiglas white using Krylon spray paint. After it had dried, I masked the track locations on the front, then

FIG. 1. TWIN-CAB SYSTEM
The BN uses a traditional twin-cab system and is operated from three control panels. One of the memory throttles (or cabs) can be plugged into a socket on either side of the panel. Power distribution to the track blocks is via the toggle switches installed in the schematic track plan.

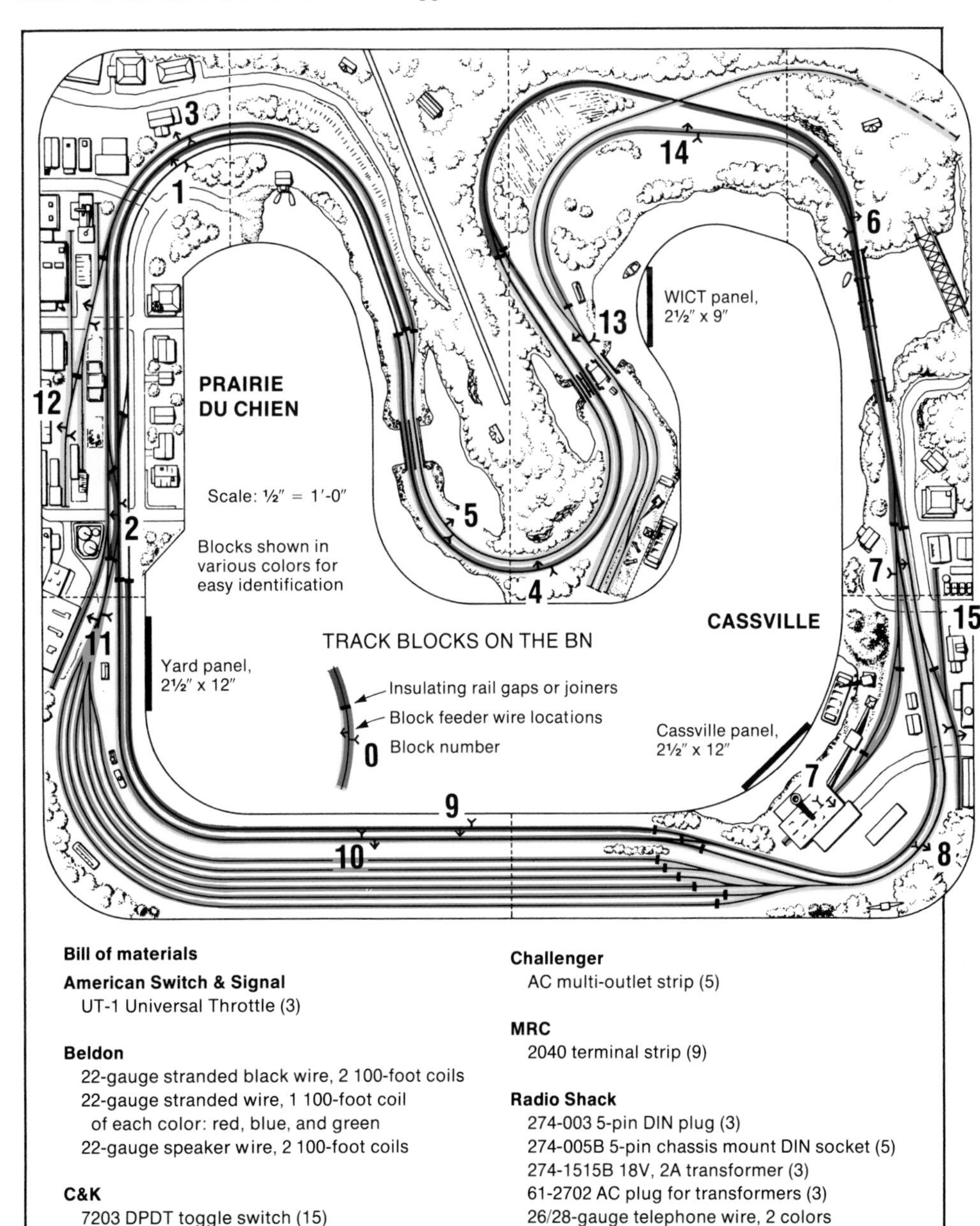

Bill of materials

American Switch & Signal
UT-1 Universal Throttle (3)

Beldon
22-gauge stranded black wire, 2 100-foot coils
22-gauge stranded wire, 1 100-foot coil of each color: red, blue, and green
22-gauge speaker wire, 2 100-foot coils

C&K
7203 DPDT toggle switch (15)

Challenger
AC multi-outlet strip (5)

MRC
2040 terminal strip (9)

Radio Shack
274-003 5-pin DIN plug (3)
274-005B 5-pin chassis mount DIN socket (5)
274-1515B 18V, 2A transformer (3)
61-2702 AC plug for transformers (3)
26/28-gauge telephone wire, 2 colors

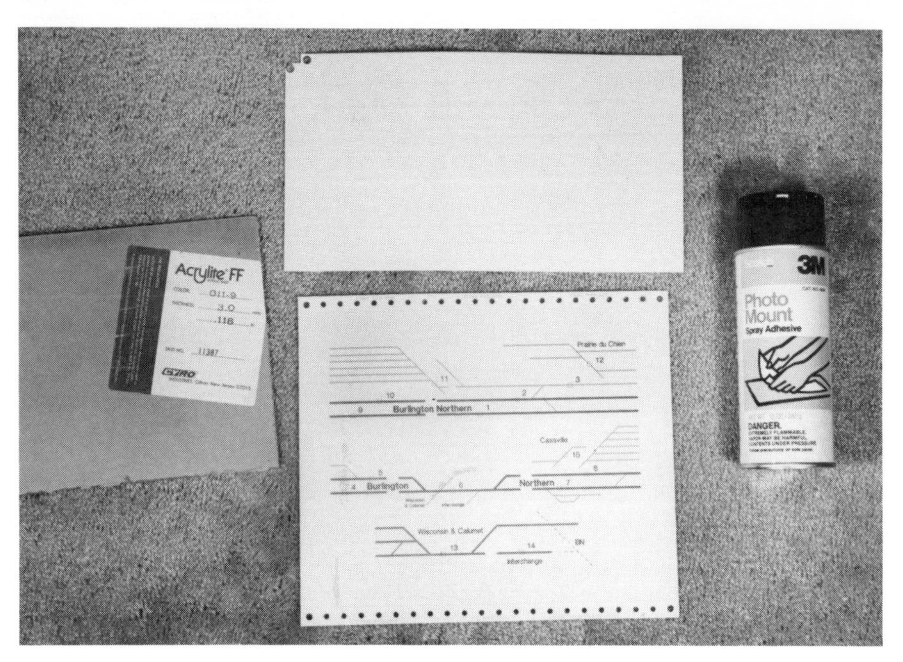

FIG. 2. SANDWICH-STYLE PANELS
Above: Here are the materials to make our layout's snazzy control panels. The artwork was generated by a computer, cemented to sheet styrene, and topped with clear Plexiglas.
Below: Toggles installed directly in the schematic make the panels user friendly.

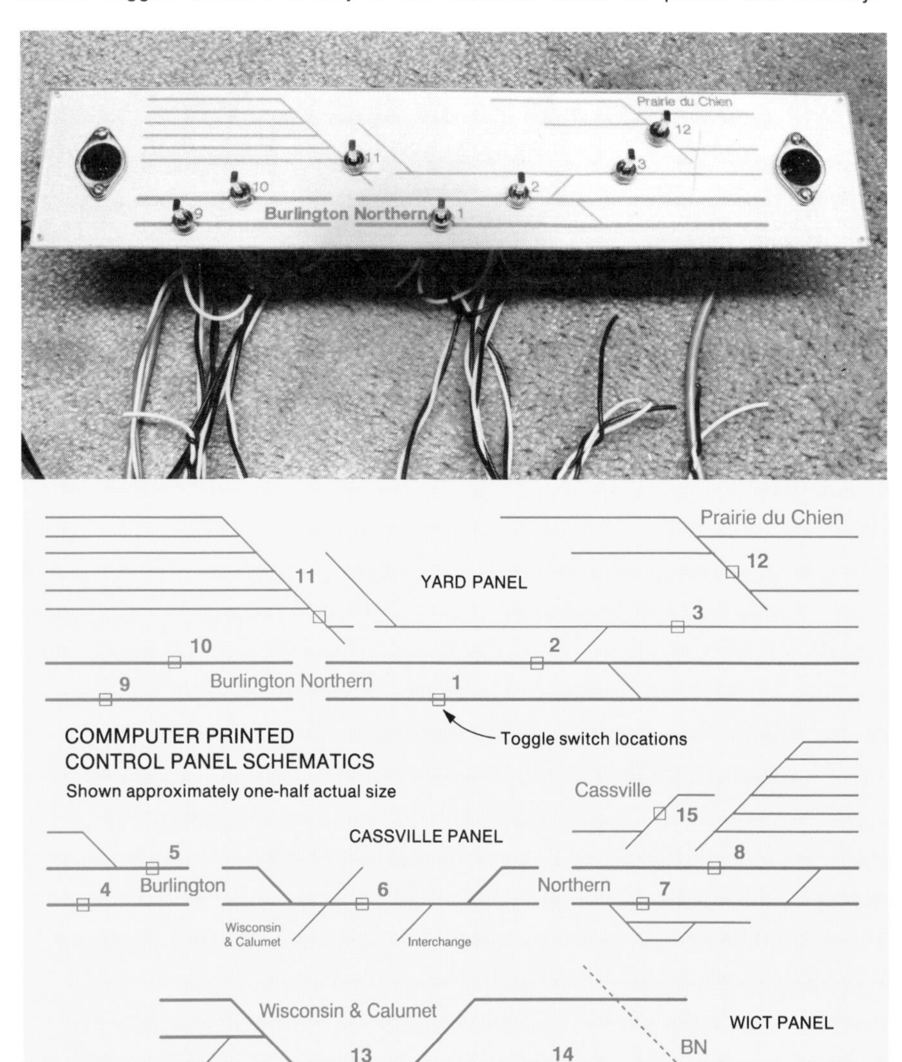

painted it dark blue. Painting both sides gave a 3-D effect that is very pleasing.

For the BN I used Plexiglas again because some was available. Time to paint it, however, was not. Trying something different, I used a drawing program on a personal computer. Before you start saying, "Ohhhhh boy, another rich kid in model railroading . . .," this method can be done easily by hand with a ruler and black ink or with colored felt-tip pens.

Figure 2 shows the materials needed to make these sandwich-style panels: ⅛"-thick, clear Plexiglas; .010" white styrene sheet; a schematic drawing; and photo-mount spray adhesive. The basic idea is to draw the control panel on paper, mount the paper to thin styrene, then cover the front with Plexiglas.

I used Freelance Plus from Lotus Development Corp. on an IBM AT with an Enhanced Graphics Adapter/Monitor and an HP Paintjet Color Printer to create the schematic for the panels. For color, a plotter works better. The software package used is not important, as any drawing program will work. A computer-aided-drafting (CAD) package would also work.

To cut the holes for the toggle switches, I used a paper punch on the paper-styrene combination. An X-acto knife with a *new* blade is good for cutting any larger hole.

For drilling holes in the Plexiglas, use the paper-styrene combo as a guide and locate the holes with a scratching tool (a sharp nail will do). Use a small drill (1/16" or 3/32") in a pin vise to further mark the center of each hole. These small indentations keep the bigger drill bit from wandering. Drill each hole using a slow to medium speed. Dulling the outer edges of the bit with a file sometimes helps eliminate cracking at the hole edges.

Holes for the five-pin DIN sockets were more difficult to cut. The proper size hole is 19/32". If you don't have a 19/32" drill, look for a 5/8"-diameter counterbore bit or a 5/8" hole saw. If you use a counterbore bit, drill from both sides so when the bit goes all the way through the last part shaved is in the center of the hole. This eliminates the chance of splintering or cracking. Also drill from both sides if you use a hole saw.

Now make the sandwich. Place the paper-styrene combo on the Plexiglas, and mount the toggle switches. See how nicely the switches hold the sandwich pieces together? Neat huh!

WIRING THE CONTROL PANELS

Since we were using terminal strips (sometimes called barrier strips) under the layout, the control panels could be prewired at the bench. That's about 1,000 percent easier than doing it upside down and backwards under the layout! See fig. 3.

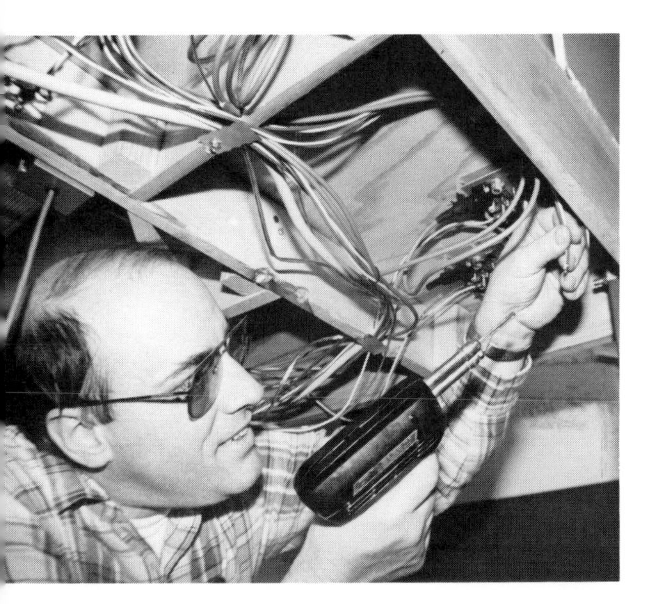

FIG. 3. ARE WE HAVING FUN YET?
Our author is soldering feeder wires under the layout. By wiring the control panels at the workbench he was able to avoid as much of this sort of unpleasantness as possible.

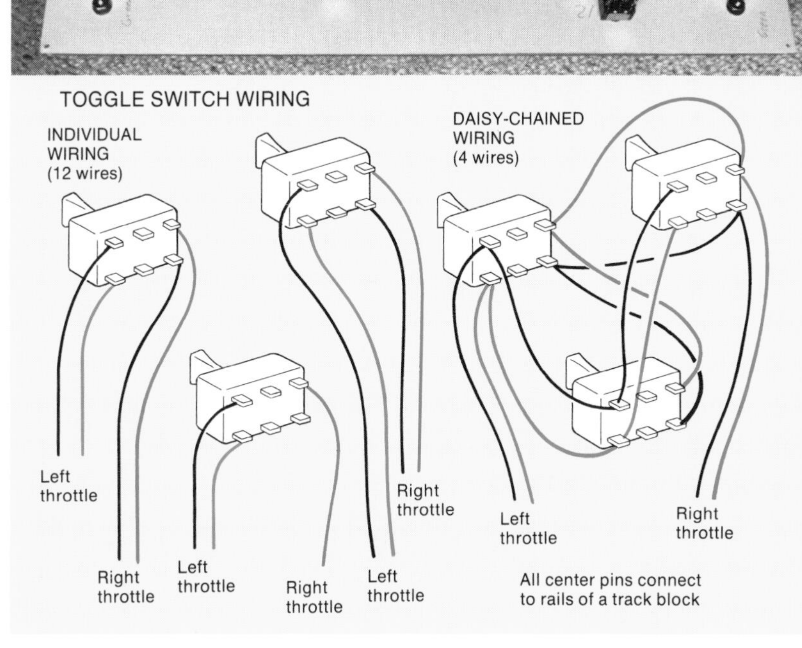

FIG. 4. WIRING CONTROL PANELS
Top right: A look at the rear of the yard control panel shows it was wired using the daisy-chain method. Wires from each pin leapfrog to corresponding pins on the other switches.

The most important item to remember in wiring is *be consistent.* Use a color code and stick to it.

When wiring a control panel at the bench, don't worry about the exact amount of wire needed — just be sure to use enough. Cut the wires 4 feet long. We used 22 gauge stranded.

Start wiring each toggle switch. You can wire the switches individually or daisy-chain them, as shown in fig. 4. Wiring each toggle switch individually is easier to understand and to troubleshoot, but daisy-chaining uses less wire and makes for a neater panel.

After you solder the wires to the toggle-switch pins, twist the pairs together and label them with a piece of tape. For example, you might use 2R for block 2 right throttle, 2L for block 2 left throttle, and 2T for block 2 track wires. You'll cut the labels off when you attach the wires to terminal strips.

The WICT panel is wired differently, as shown in fig. 5. The interchange track can be controlled from the WICT throttle or either of the two mainline throttles, whichever one has control of block 6, the single-track main line.

To wire the throttle sockets and plugs, use the wire that came with the throttles. We didn't need throttle tethers 10 feet long, so we cut them into two pieces, one 6 feet long, the other 4. The six-footers became our tethers. We used the shorter lengths under the layout to connect the control units to the terminal strips.

To mount the control panels cut rectangular holes in the framework large enough to accommodate the toggle switches and five-pin DIN connectors. Secure the panels with small screws.

Mount the terminal strips under the layout, close to the panels (see fig. 6). The location doesn't make much difference; the number of terminal connections does. Connect the labeled wires from the panel to the right spot in the terminal strips.

Follow the throttle instructions for installing them. Figure 7 shows the schematic relationship of the throttle control units, the terminal strips, and the yard control panel.

TRACK WIRING

For feeder wires to the track use a small size telephone wire, typically 26- or 28-gauge solid wire. These wires should be 3" to 6" long, just enough to get under the layout and attach to a stranded wire.

Use a $^1/_{16}$" bit to drill access holes between two ties on the outside of each rail. Do *not* drill the two holes exactly

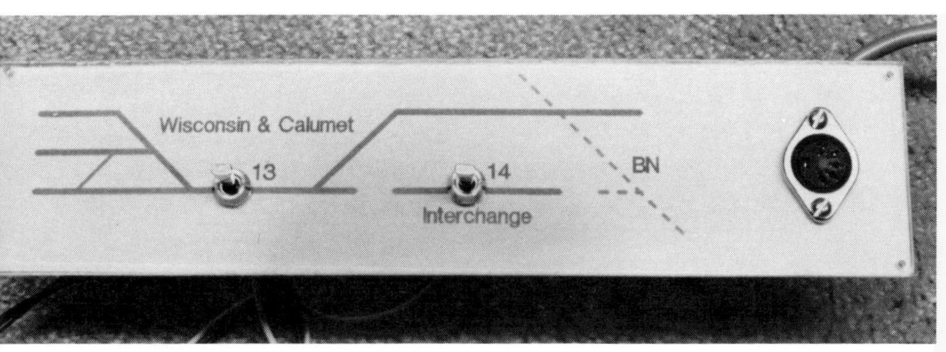

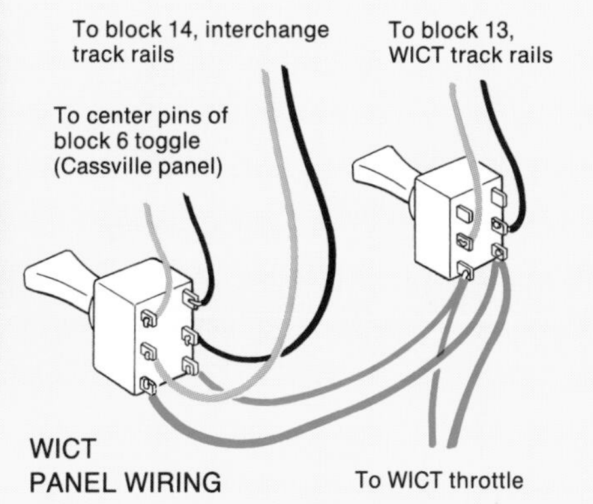

FIG. 5. WICT PANEL WIRING
Block 13 can be controlled by only the WICT throttle. Block 14, the interchange track, can be controlled by a mainline throttle also controlling block 6 or by the WICT throttle.

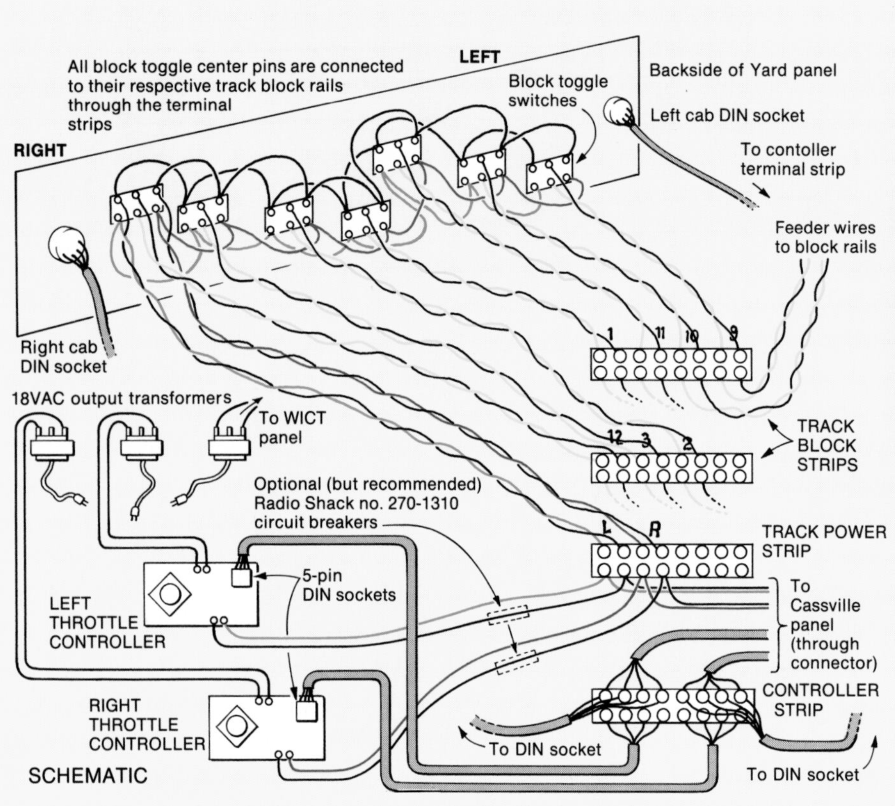

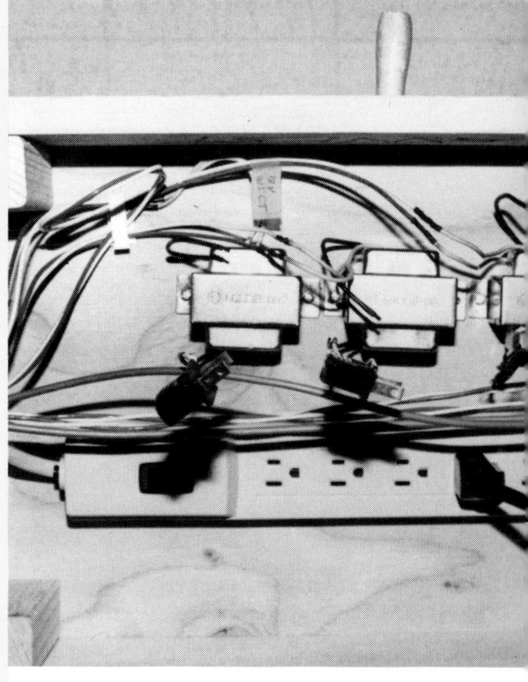

FIG. 7. THROTTLE INSTALLATION
Above: Each throttle requires its own transformer. These are mounted under the tabletop and plug

opposite each other. Sometimes the track gauge narrows when soldering the wires to the rail, so offset the two wires by an inch or so. See fig. 8.

Once again, color-coding is important. Use one color for the "outside" rail (the one closest to the backdrop)

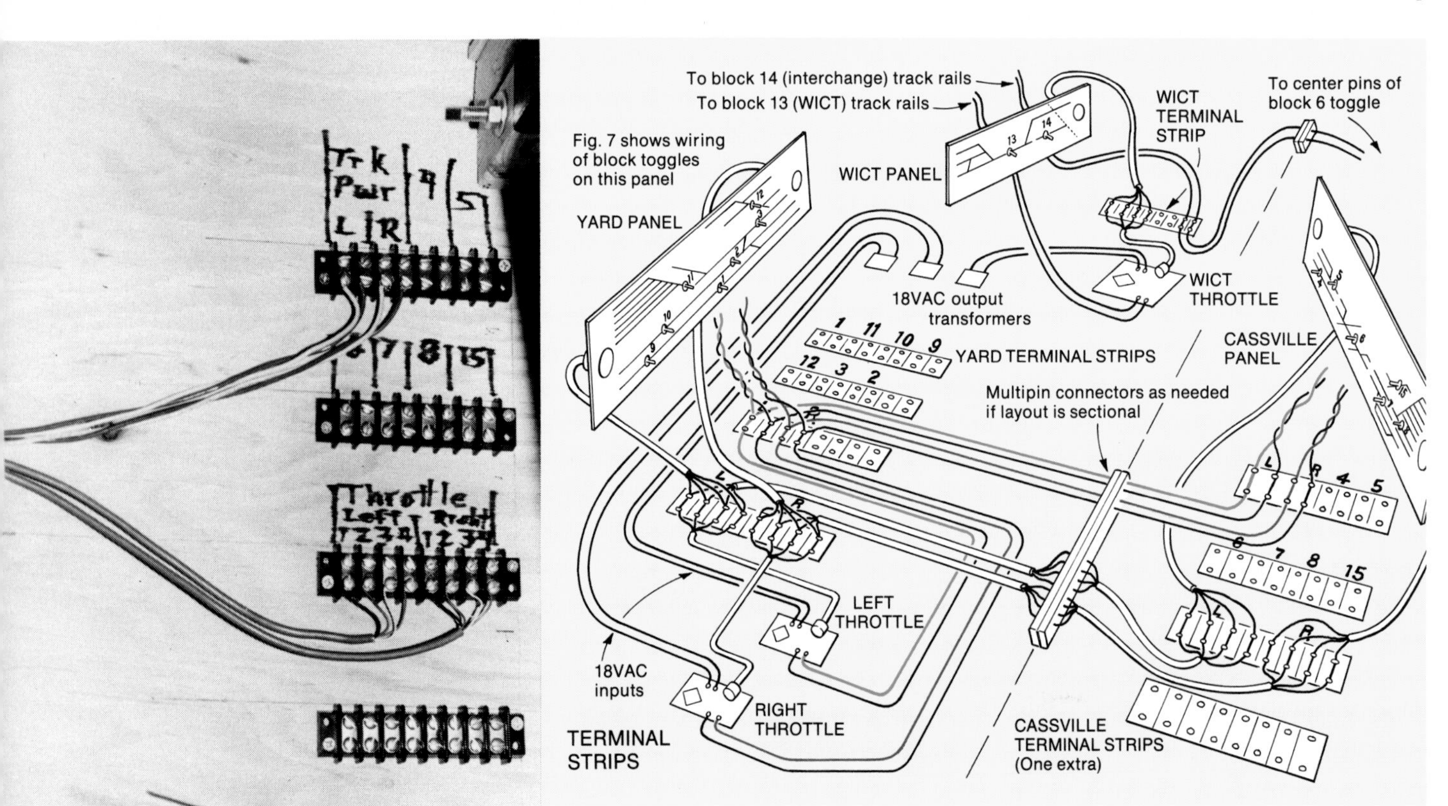

FIG. 6. TERMINAL STRIPS
Using terminal strips makes wiring easier and also greatly simplifies troubleshooting. Our Madison crew screwed them to the undersides of the plywood tabletops near the control panels.

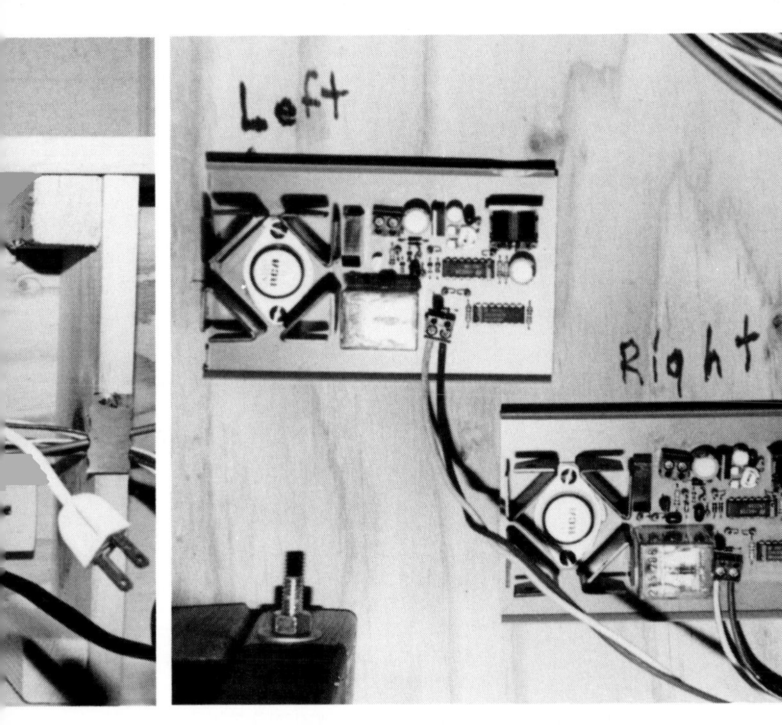

into an adjacent plug strip. Note that layout frame members are notched on the bottom. Wires are held in the notches by metal strips, protected from damage if modules are lying on floor. **Right:** Printed-circuit boards for the throttles are also mounted to the bottom of the layout.

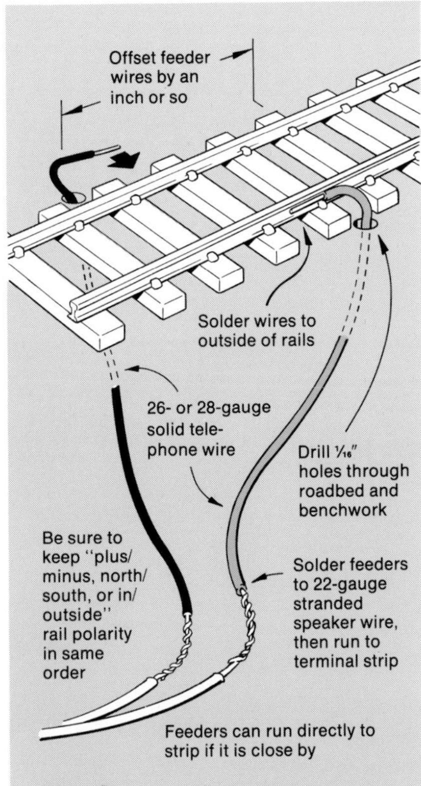

Fig. 8 ATTACHING FEEDER WIRES

and another color for the "inside" rail. From each set of track-access wires, run a color-coded pair of wires back to the terminal strips. We used 20-gauge stranded speaker wire with one wire gold and one silver, designating the gold to be equivalent to black. Allow some slack if you plan to use connectors between layout sections.

With the wiring completed, the area around the terminal strips can look very messy. Bundling the wires coming out of each side of the strips will make the wiring a lot neater.

CHECKING IT OUT

Now that the layout is wired, it's time to check it out! Place an engine on the track, turn on the power and pray! Run the engine from block to block. The engine should continue in the same direction as it crosses block boundaries. If it doesn't there is a problem with the block. Usually the inside/outside wires are reversed.

If you are building the layout so it can be easily taken apart, leave about a foot of slack in each wire that passes under a joint between modules. To determine what type of connector to use, simply add up the number of wires that cross the boundary and find a connector or combination of connectors that has at least that many pins. Computer DB-25 connectors are good for this. They have 25 pins. The same type also comes in 9-, 15-, and 50-pin variations.

To wire the connectors, cut a wire and connect one end to pin 1 of the male connector and the other end to pin 1 of the female connector. Cut the next wire and connect each of its ends to pin 2 of the male and female connectors. Continue until all the wires have been connected. See, it really is one wire at a time!

EVALUATION

The walkaround memory throttles are great even for a small layout like this. If we had used tethered throttles with 10-foot cables, we would have hanged ourselves by now! The shorter, 6-foot cables don't get tangled up and still allow the operator to get next to the train, anywhere on the layout. With the memory feature you can disconnect your throttle from the yard panel, walk over to the Cassville panel and plug it in — all while your train keeps moving.

Next month we'll show you how to ballast the track, so see you then! ✪

Ballasting track on the N scale Burlington Northern

Homemade spreading tools make the job a lot easier

Color photos by A. L. Schmidt

Above: Here's Crawford Junction on our N scale Burlington Northern, a 9 x 10-foot railroad introduced in our February 1990 issue. It's at Crawford that the mighty Burlington Northern crosses the humble Wisconsin & Calumet. The BN's ballast is beautifully groomed granite, whereas the little ballast remaining on the Wicket is overgrown with weeds. **Below:** A short northbound BN freight sweeps into Prairie du Chien. The structures seen here are faithful to the prototype and were described in last month's MR.

BY ED HAMMER

PHOTOS BY THE BN BUILDERS

THIS MONTH we'll ballast the track on our N scale project railroad. It would take a better salesman than me to convince folks that ballasting is fun, but having a group of modelers working on it together does make the job a lot easier. And the results are wonderful — our toy-like tracks are magically transformed into a real railroad.

CHOOSING COLORS

On our field trips to the Prairie du Chien area, we took closeup color photos of the track for later study. The ballast on the Burlington Northern's twin main line, we discovered, was a combination of gray and pink granite. In fact, the pink looked to me just like the rock that comes from the Chicago & North Western's Pink Lady Quarry at Rock Springs, Wis.

Both BN mains showed evidence of long-term oil leakage from the diesels running the route. Additionally, the southbound track was littered with Milk Duds-sized iron-ore pellets from the unit taconite trains traveling from northern Minnesota to the smelter at Granite City, Ill.

After considerable study of the photos and experimentation, we arrived at the ballast blends shown in the accompanying table. Probably you won't have any real Pink Lady, but you can use a commercially available pink.

Our real Pink Lady was compliments of the Mid-Continent Railway Museum at North Freedom, Wis., which let me borrow several small buckets of it. This started as fine-graded material that the C&NW can't use and must dispose of. The museum is happy to accept and use it. Too fine for the C&NW is still way too coarse for N scale, though, so my wife and I sifted the material through strainers and filled our buckets with only the finest of the fine.

You'll recall that our layout actually features two railroads, the second one being the Wisconsin & Calumet. The "Wicket" is a former Milwaukee Road branch that saw minimal maintenance for many years and could stand a major rehabilitation, including new ballast and ties. Dirt and weeds cover the little ballast that remains. For the Wicket we decided to use a light gray that would peek nicely through the ground foam weeds.

DISTRIBUTING THE BALLAST

"Good grief," you ask, "when do we get on with actually laying some ballast?" Well, if you'll recall, we've already done some. Back in the May issue we ballasted the turnouts before actually laying them. This worked great, and we heartily recommend it. Just cover the backs of the turnouts with electrical tape, sprinkle on some ballast, tamp it in, and then dump off the excess.

As shown in fig. 1, we used masking tape to cover the switch points, going two or three ties beyond the switch point ends. This will help keep ballast and glue out of the points. Then we painted the track with an airbrush.

We mixed up enough ballast to get a good start, using a plastic margarine tub to hold it. To dispense the ballast we used small (less than 1 teaspoon) measuring spoons. Teaspoons also work well for those of you with steadier hands. See fig. 2. Just don't use your spouse's finest flatware; go out and purchase some cheap plastic measuring spoons.

Try to spread the ballast with a rocking or shaking motion that will cause those teeny stones to fall out uniformly. Alternatively, tap the spoon with a finger from your other hand to help shake the ballast out.

Ballast rarely extends above the top of the ties. Usually it's one to several inches below. On this stretch of the heavily trafficked BN, however, you'd be hard pressed to find any area on the main line where the ballast doesn't peek over the tie tops. The BN can't afford to let this heavy-tonnage main line deteriorate in the slightest. Every time one of our group went to look at the project area, the track gangs or their efforts were highly visible.

SPREADING THE BALLAST

Once the ballast is applied you need to level it. You can accomplish this with a soft brush, some ballast spreaders, or a combination of these.

We tried some of the ballast spreaders on the market, but got better results with our homemade ones, also shown in fig. 2. Jack Hillebrandt fabricated these from blocks of wood and some .040"-thick sheet styrene. You can easily make your own. The groove depths will depend upon the height of the rail you use.

Notice the concave shape on the front of the tools. This works the ballast away from the rail sides, where it can stick and cause derailments. Incidentally, you're always better off to be a little short of ballast. Adding more is much easier than trying to remove excess.

Once the ballast has been spread we use small paintbrushes for any final smoothing. Tamiya no. 3 flat horsehair brushes worked for us, but there are others that should work as well.

BONDING THE BALLAST

We used Dave Frary's *How to Build Realistic Model Railroad Scenery*, published by Kalmbach, as our "scenery bible." He recommends wetting the ballast with wet water before applying diluted glue, so that's what we did.

For wet water Frary suggests 1 pint of warm water and 4 drops of a wetting agent such as liquid dishwashing detergent. To that we added a little isopropyl alcohol, and this seemed to work very well. The wetting agent reduces the water's surface tension, allowing it to soak into the ballast quickly.

We sprayed our wet water from spray bottles like the one shown in fig. 3. We prefer trigger-type bottles, like this one, to pumpers. You can squeeze the trigger with several fingers, while with the pump you'll use only one. That one can get mighty tired!

Apply the wet water liberally. This will enable the diluted white glue to soak into all the ballast, not just part of it. When the wet water starts to puddle you've gotten your ballast well soaked.

Don't hold the spray bottle too close to the ballast, or you'll blow it around before it gets a chance to get wet. And

Ballast blends used

BN main lines
- 4 parts dark gray
- 4 parts Pink Lady
- 1 part black
- 1 part buff

Industrial sidings
- 2 parts cinders
- 1 part buff
- 1 part dark gray

Staging yard
- 3 parts dark gray
- 1 part buff
- 1 part cinders

Wisconsin & Calumet
- Light gray

FIG. 1. PAINTING THE TRACK
Above: The turnouts were painted and ballasted before installation. Here masking tape has been added to help keep glue out of the points. **Right:** All the track was painted before ballasting. It's a good idea to wear a protective mask and use a fan or two to exhaust the air to the outdoors.

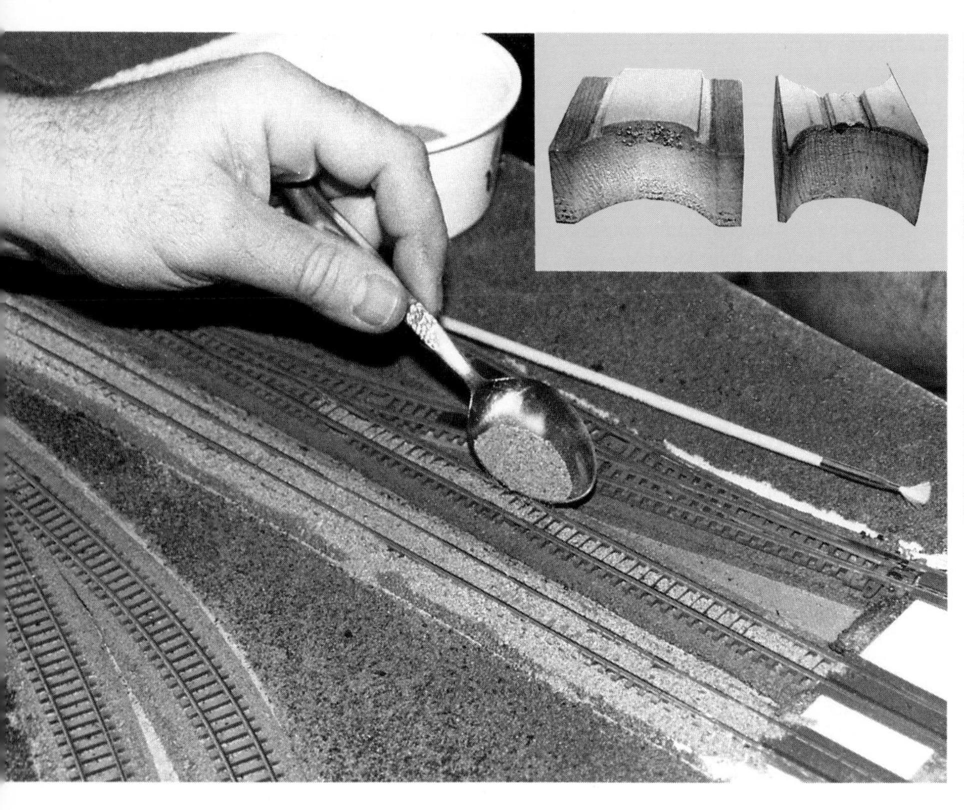

FIG. 2. SPREADING BALLAST
Left: Ballast was distributed with spoons, preferably not nice ones like the one seen here. Shown in the inset are two homemade spreaders used to shape and smooth the ballast. The one on the left is for working between parallel tracks; the other is for between the rails. **Above:** Here's a ballast spreader in action. Touch-up can be done with a soft, flat brush.

once the ballast does become wet it's about impossible to smooth.

NEXT COMES THE GLUE

I hope you've saved some of your old white glue bottles, as they make great dispensers. We usually mix the 50:50 ratio of diluted white glue in those 8- or 16-ounce bottles. To that mix, we add two capfuls of isopropyl alcohol.

Then we use the glue dispenser to drip the diluted white glue onto the ballast. If the mixture flows too freely, simply turn the cap down partway.

Be careful not to use too much diluted white glue near switch points. Wet water makes the glue flow quite freely, so it's easy to glue the points shut.

FIG. 3. WETTING AND BONDING
Below: Wow, this is fun! For best results you need to shoot a fine mist of wet water and let it settle down over the ballast like a gentle N scale rain. Otherwise the grooming will go for nought. **Right:** Emptied white glue bottles make excellent glue applicators.

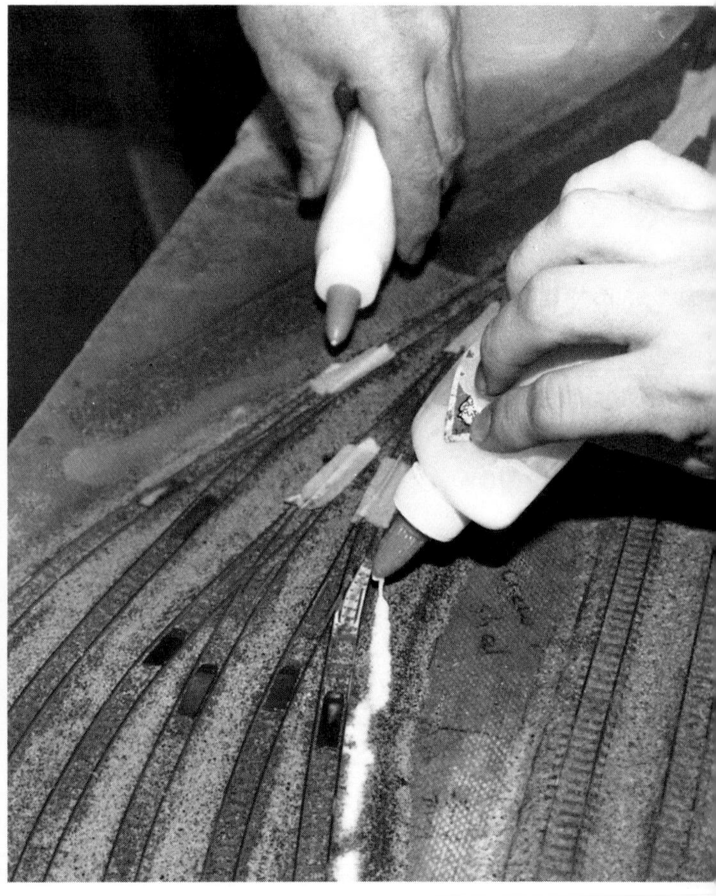

You can tell when you've applied enough glue by the way the mixture is absorbed into the ballast — it'll puddle as the ballast becomes saturated. That's your signal to cease and desist.

If you apply too little glue, all the ballast will not be bonded. A crust will form on top, with loose ballast underneath, and it'll start to come off when you move the layout around, when you use your shop vac to remove the dust and grime from track-cleaning operations, or when your hand touches the ballast while rerailing an engine or car. If that happens, go back and touch up certain areas, as is shown in fig. 4.

Apparently we had better luck than Mr. Frary with diluted white glue — he prefers matte medium. We used white glue almost exclusively for applying all ballast, texture, and lichen, and we did not find an objectionable shine. In fact, we used more than a gallon of white glue on the railroad. (That's for everything though, not just ballasting.) One of the interesting things about this hobby is that what works for one may not work for the next.

CLEARING TURNOUT POINTS

As you're ballasting you should return to the turnouts from time to time to see that the points are still working properly. It's far easier to work on them at this stage while the glue is still wet or only partially hardened. Make certain that the turnout operates freely and snaps into position without interference from the ballast or glue. Work the points back and forth several times; if necessary, soak up the excess white glue with paper toweling.

If you do glue a switch shut, don't panic. The white glue we're using is water soluble. Just give those points a bath with wet water, let them soak for a while, then work them free, and clean them out.

A few years from now, when you want to realign part of your track, you'll thank yourself over and over again for having used white glue. All you have to do is soak the track with wet water. Before long the track, ballast, and cork roadbed will come free. Then you'll be able to recycle the track, at least.

"How much track can I ballast in an evening?" you may ask. Well, our best guess is that one person should be able to complete 10 to 15 feet of track in about three hours.

Once the glue has dried, feel free to pull out the track nails. (Even though we didn't.) The glue is more than capable of holding the track in place.

Take your time, and have some of your favorite background music playing. Next month's get-together will conclude this series, so appropriately enough, the subject will be finishing touches!

FIG. 4. TOUCHING UP

Top: Low spots alongside details or ties can be filled with a little extra ballast. **Above:** The area can be smoothed with a soft brush. **Below:** Apply a little bit of glue, and all is well.

The N scale Burlington Northern: Conclusion

We finish the project railroad

Roads, water, scenery, and lots of little things that count

BY ED HAMMER
PHOTOS BY THE BN BUILDERS

YES FRIENDS, there's light at the end of the tunnel. In this, the last (no applause, please!) installment of our N scale Burlington Northern series, we'll take a look at finishing touches on our 9 x 10-foot railroad.

ROADS AND STREETS

For roads on flat plywood areas, we started with cork roadbed as the base (fig. 1). To this we cemented .010"-thick styrene cut roughly 20 scale feet wide. We used rubber cement as the adhesive, applying two coats on the cork because of its porous texture and one on the styrene. After letting the cement dry, we pressed the surfaces together for a contact bond.

We painted the styrene Grimy Black, using a no. 3 Tamiya brush. Once the surface had dried, the roadway was striped with 1/32" Formaline colored tapes for the center and edge lines.

To construct roads and streets in areas where Sculptamold provided the hills and hillsides, we simply smoothed more Sculptamold over the road area with a putty knife, building it up to the approximate roadway elevation and letting it dry. Then we glued cork roadbed to the Sculptamold, not being overly concerned about whether the roadbed exhibited some minor "rolling" — many finished roadways do that in real life.

And what's a road without a guardrail — a dangerous road, that's what!

FIG. 1. MODELING ROADS
Above: Highways were built up with cork roadbed, then surfaced with sheet styrene. **Upper right:** The styrene surfaces were worked into the shoulders with spackling compound. **Right:** The roads were painted Grimy Black, then the ground was added.

A. L. Schmidt

Left: Our layout is set in the southwest corner of "America's Dairyland," so it seems only reasonable that our Holstein and Guernsey citizens should be well represented. The Burlington Northern train, Mini-Trix U28s on the point, is just north of Crawford Junction, where the BN interchanges with the Wisconsin & Calumet. This walk-in style N scale layout was introduced in our February issue. **Above:** This little beach outside Prairie du Chien is a very pleasant place to spend a summer afternoon. On the hillside you can see two of the billboards made using photos taken during field trips to the modeled area. And yes, there really is a Pizza Hut on the south side of Prairie du Chien.

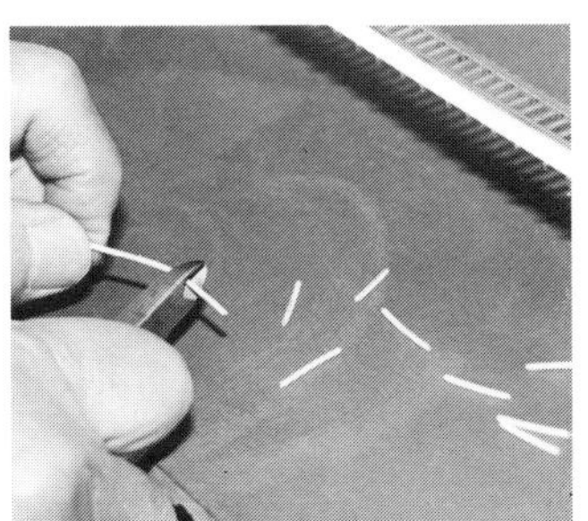

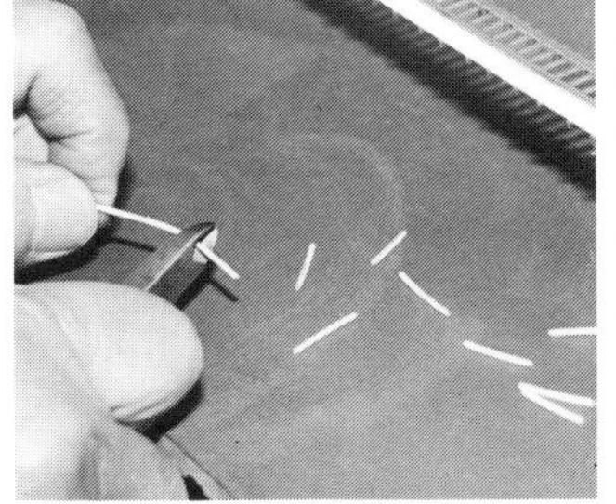

FIG. 2. HIGHWAY GUARDRAILS

Above: The guardrail posts were cut from no. 24 insulated wire. **Below left:** Holes were drilled for the posts, using a homemade gauge for spacing. **Above right:** The posts were dipped in white glue and cemented in, projecting 1/8" above the ground. A spoon or bottle cap makes a handy glue holder for dipping. **Below right:** To finish the job, a single .020" x .060" styrene guardrail was cemented on with CA. Again, note the use of a spacing gauge to locate the guardrail the proper distance above the ground for a neater job.

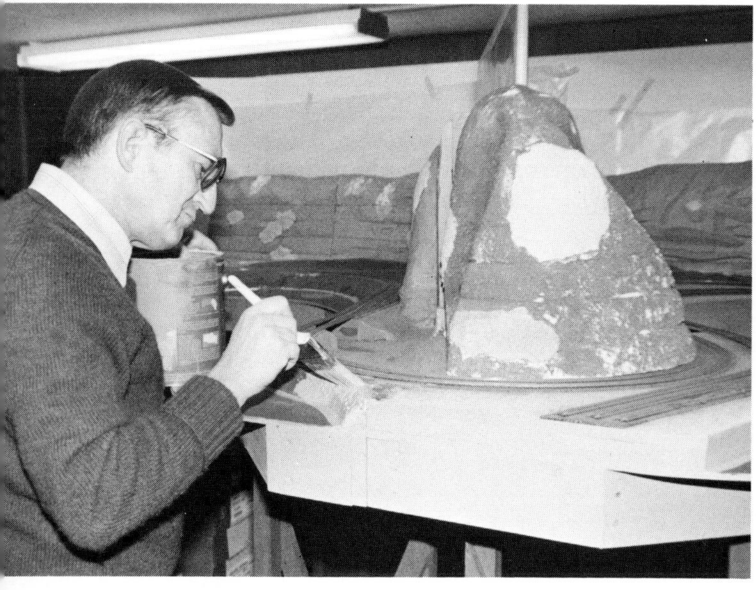

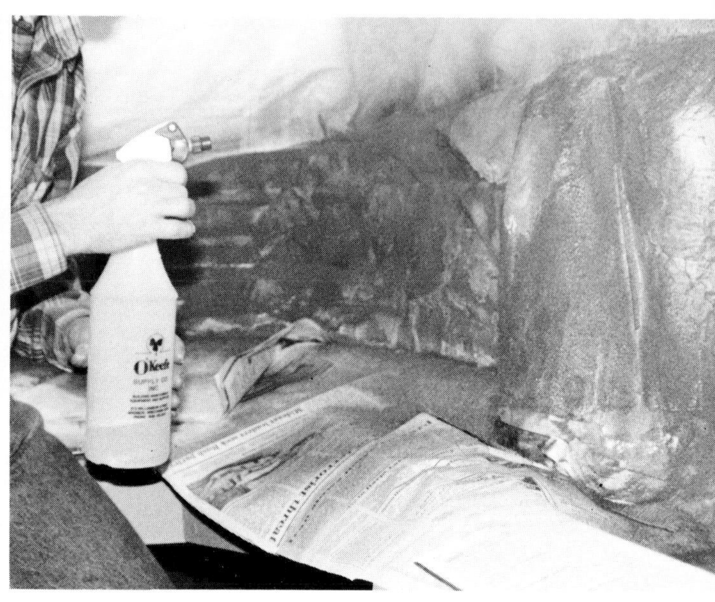

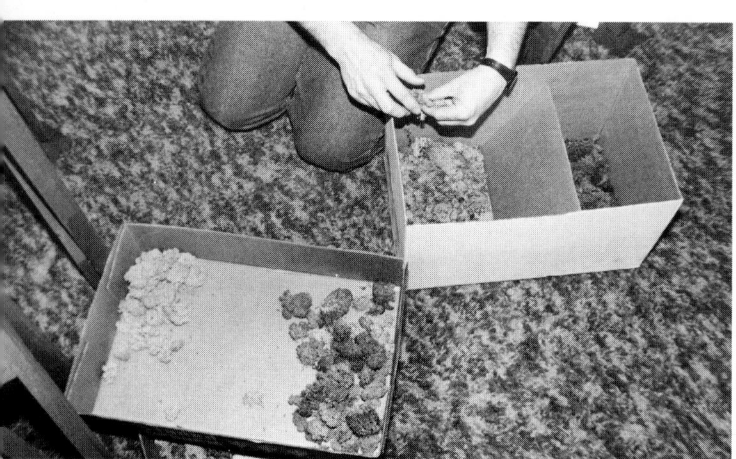

FIG. 4. LICHEN

Left: Lichen from several manufacturers was sorted and mixed. **Above left:** Clump by clump it was dipped in white glue and applied to the layout. **Above right:** Wooden toothpicks helped hold the lichen in place on the hill-sides. **Right:** Lichen planting was a no-holds-barred, people-intensive drill.

FIG. 5. TONING IT DOWN

Left: A majority of the modelers decided the lichen was too bright. To tone it down it was first sprayed with dilute matte medium. **Below left:** Then green ground foam was sprinkled on lightly.

FIG. 6. CARVING ROCKS

Rock faces were made by carving strata into wet Sculptamold with a knife.

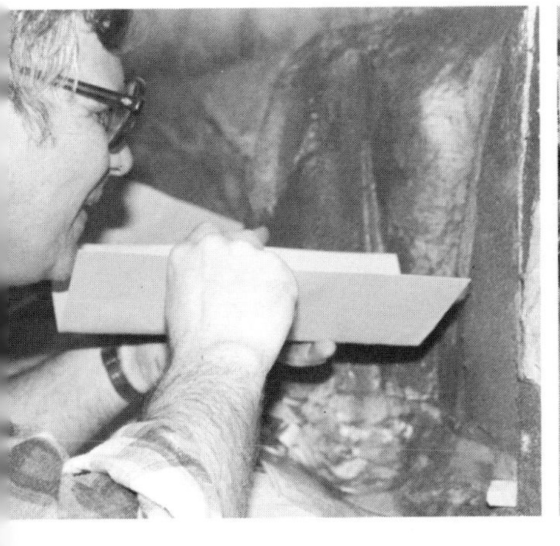

FIG. 3. GROUND COVER
Far left: Ground on the layout was painted with tan latex paint. **Left:** The bluff faces were wet with a spray bottle. Then a mixture of ground foam and dry glue was sprinkled on, and the surfaces were sprayed some more. **Above left:** The foam was blown into vertical surfaces. **Above right:** The crew members nearly hyperventilated, so an air hose was brought to the rescue.

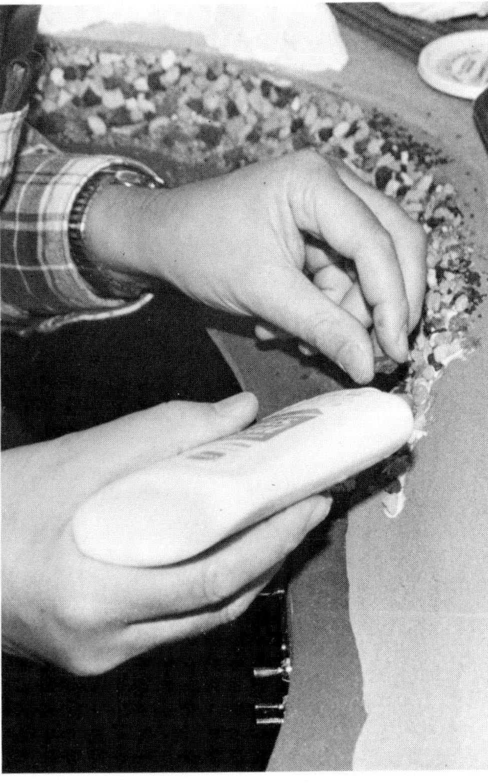

FIG. 7. ADDING RIPRAP
Above: At some places along the riverbank (the power plant for example), erosion cannot be risked and is prevented by reinforcing the shore with large rocks. How better to represent these big rocks than with small ones? **Right:** The group had a considerable assortment of rocks, which they glued on one by one. Yes, it got a tad tedious.

Figure 2 shows how we added these essential safety features.

FINISHED SCENERY

For grass and earth, we used Woodland Scenics ground foam, mixed in a variety of grades and colors. See fig. 3. To these mixes we added an equal amount of powdered glue, also by Woodland Scenics. Generally we'd wet the layout, sprinkle on some foam, then wet it some more, so as to dissolve and activate the glue. It would be difficult to add too much texture to a layout, so we used liberal quantities of these materials.

Don't forget plantings around the building foundations, and yes, ivy crawling up the building sides.

And then there was the lichen, lots and lots of it, as shown in fig. 4. Once the fall foliage was in place, the majority of our crew judged it to be too bright. So, as shown in fig. 5, we toned it down with ground foam.

To represent rock surfaces on the layout, we carved wet Sculptamold, as shown in fig. 6. And talk about your torture tests, fig. 7 shows how we built riprap banks where needed on the river.

You could build up a coal pile by pouring bag after bag of scale coal until you were done. Certainly it would be authentic, but fig. 8 shows a far easier way.

MODELING WATER

Step one in modeling the muddy Mississippi was painting the plywood river bottom. We used an airbrush and painted lighter colors near the shore, feathering them into the black used to represent deeper water.

For the water itself we used Enviro-Tex, a two-part epoxy available at hardware stores (fig. 9). Before pouring the epoxy we stapled strips of posterboard along the outside of the layout to form a temporary dam. We used 2″ duct tape to seal the seams between adjacent strips of the posterboard.

This arrangement didn't prevent all leaks of the Enviro-Tex, but did slow them down enough that we could "manage" them into buckets or onto newspapers. We made two pours for a total thickness of about 1/8″. The directions warn about coming in contact with the material, so we wore rubber gloves.

THE COAL BARGES

Dennis Pehoski scratchbuilt the two coal barges, using sheet and strip styrene. The prototypes are 35 x 195 feet, but Dennis made his 25 x 135 to fit the river areas available on the layout. See fig. 10. He drew plans using diagrams from the Cassville River Terminal Co. and his own photos. We wanted two coal barges, one loaded and one empty, so Dennis used a draft chart provided by the company to determine the heights of the barges above the waterline. Last

FIG. 8. COAL PILES
Above: The piles were built from chunks of foam and contoured with Sculptamold. **Right:** Next came black paint and scale coal.

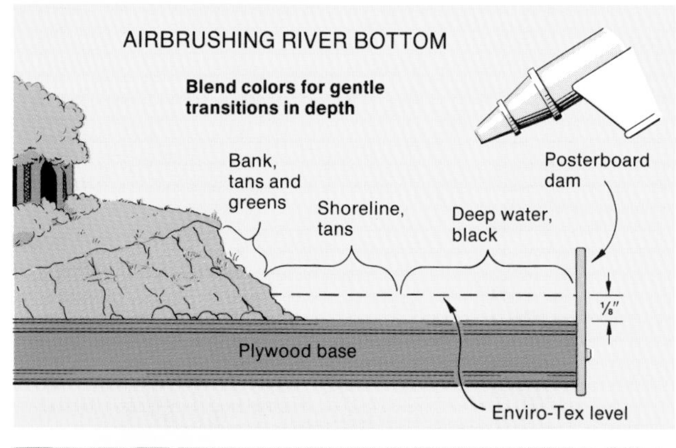

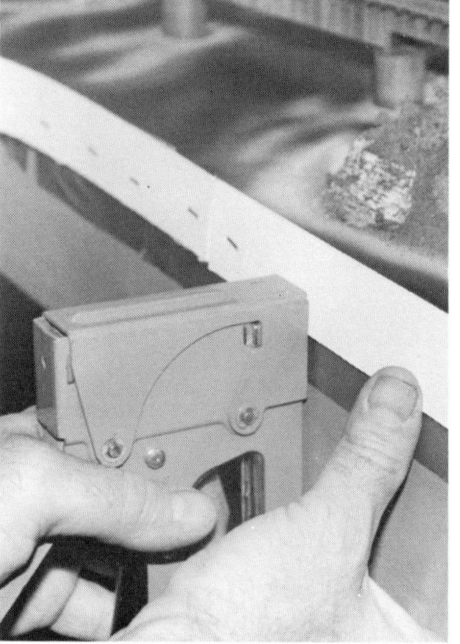

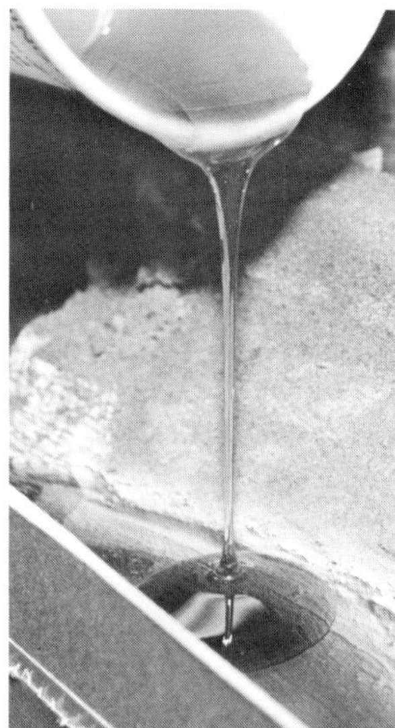

FIG. 9. MODELING WATER
Upper left: The water area was airbrushed with tan and some greens in shallow areas, feathered out to black for deep water. **Above left:** A temporary cardboard dam was stapled along the edges of the water area. Duct tape was added to seal off any leaks under the cardboard. **Above right:** Water was represented with Enviro-Tex, a two-part epoxy. When poured it has about the consistency of honey, but will leak anywhere there's even a pinhole opening. **Left:** Following the product's directions, the Enviro-Tex was gone over with an air hose to flow it into nooks and crannies, meanwhile working out bubbles.

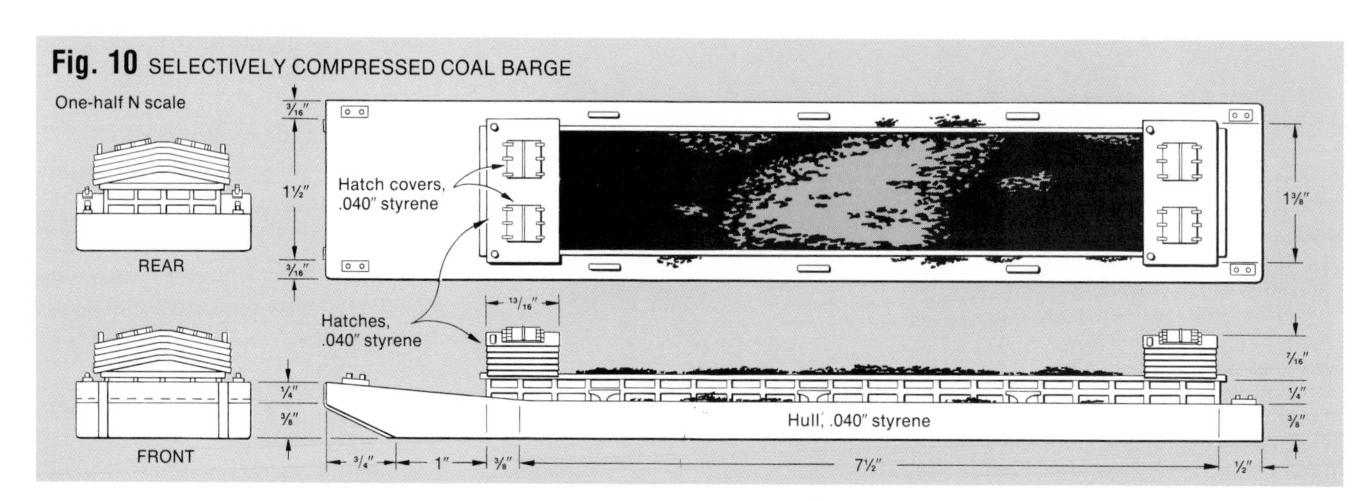

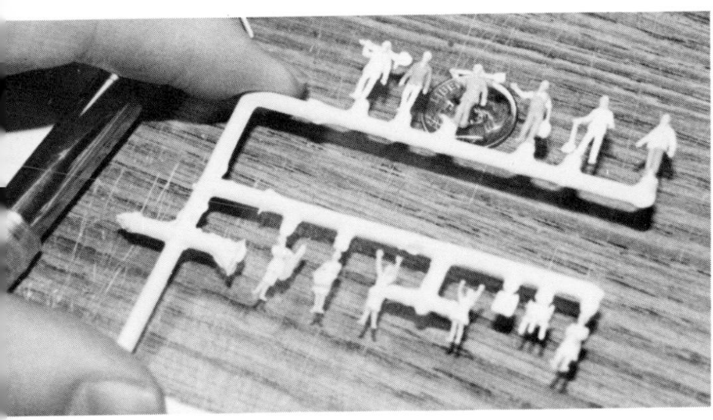

FIG. 11. PAINTING FIGURES
Even a small layout can absorb hundreds of figures, so one economical way to buy them is in unpainted sets from Preiser. You can modify them easily, and that one little guy you can never find in the painted sets is probably on that undecorated sprue.

Fig. 12
Truck bed, from Bachmann set 7011
Rotating beacon, Loco-Motives 2030
Cab, Con-Cor Kenworth
Kadee Z scale railroad wheels
Auto chassis, from Bachmann set 7020

FIG. 12. BN MAINTENANCE TRUCK
A truck similar to this would make a nice detail for just about any N scaler's layout. Track crews use it for all kinds of jobs.

month's installment included some good closeup shots of the barges.

I also want to thank Mr. Ray "Chico" Lawrence of the Cassville River Terminal Co. for providing some valuable information on barge traffic.

Besides hosting the loaded barge, our WICT coal docks are home to a Stewart no. 1200 25-ton crane, but we converted it by leaving off the short flatcar base and substituting a set of crawler tracks from the backhoe included in a Micro Machines no. 22 construction set. This came from a toy store but suitably sized crawler tracks off anything would be fine.

PAINTING MINIATURE FIGURES

We bought unpainted figures from Preiser and used nos. 00, 0 and 1 brushes to paint them with acrylics. A magnifying glass with a built-in light was also helpful. We chose acrylics because they're easy to use and clean up and so many colors are available, including metallics (fig. 11). [Our crew used Duncan Bisq-Stain paints, available in half-ounce bottles at craft stores and hobby shops. Small bottles of military colors by Tamiya and other manufacturers could also be used. — *Ed.*]

For ease of handling, leave the figures on the sprue. If you have a small modeling vise with a head that swivels, you'll find that very handy in holding the sprues. If you don't have a small vise, steady hands will get you by.

Start painting with the flesh colors. You can add other colors to attempt slight changes in the texture, tone, or coloring of the flesh tones. Then paint the clothes. Leave the hair for last; when you finally detach the figure from the sprue you can grasp it by the feet to finish painting the head.

Remember that the figures are small; you can't add much detail — facial or otherwise. Try simulating a hard hat by painting the person's head white, yellow, or silver, but make sure you let a little hair peek out from underneath.

Acrylic paints dry very fast. If you don't like your results, simply try again while the figure is still in front of you. You'll find that with a little practice, you should be able to paint the 100 or so figures in a Preiser assorted figure set in a single afternoon.

THE BN RAIL RIDER CRANE

See fig. 12 for this neat railroad maintenance truck. Dennis Pehoski put his nimble fingers to work again to produce this jewel, starting with a Kenworth tractor from the Con-Cor tractor-trailer set.

Before assembling the truck Dennis painted the parts with Scalecoat II. The BN emblems came from a Microscale BN 45-foot trailer decal set.

Speaking of trucks, we seldom saw a tractor with a sleeper cab on it in the area we modeled, so George Nelson removed the sleeper and shortened the wheelbase of most of these vehicles.

SIGNS AND BILLBOARDS

Several of the buildings have colored signs, and there are also four colored billboards advertising Prairie du Chien area services. Nearly all these signs originated as color photographs and were reduced to an appropriate size on a color copier.

I used the color copier facilities at Econoprint here in Madison. Their machine is a Canon color laser copier, which can reduce copies to 50 percent and enlarge them to 400 percent of original size, each in a single step. To reduce a photo or drawing to a size smaller then 50 percent, say 45 percent, find the square root of that number on your electronic slide ruler (calculator) and copy it twice at that figure.

Let's take the 45 percent reduction as an example. The approximate square root of 45 percent (0.45) is 67 percent (0.67). Copy the first reduction at 67 percent, then make a 67 percent copy of the first copy. Since 0.67 multiplied by 0.67 equals 0.4489, that's close enough to 0.45 or 45 percent.

BLOCK SIGNALS

We use block signals on this layout to protect the single-track main line that crosses the Wisconsin River.

Figure 13 shows how we made these working signals, starting with Bachmann's inexpensive plastic models. We removed the plastic ladders and replaced the plastic lenses with green and red light-emitting diodes (LEDs) in the signal head, running the wire leads down behind the mast. A brass ladder improved the appearance of the signal and helped hide the wires.

As the drawing shows, we used a 560-ohm resistor on the wire from the red LED and a 240-ohm resistor on the wire from the green. This was because we found that the green LED required almost twice the current to achieve the same light intensity. The LEDs are

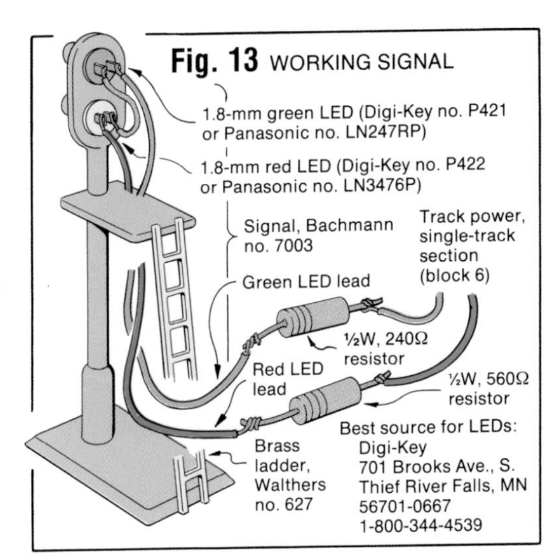

powered directly off the track power, so the lights change when the polarity changes. Pretty neat, huh? If your throttle has control of the block and your direction switch is set to cross the bridge, you'll get the green light.

The second signal is built the same way, but because it faces the opposite direction its track power connections are the opposite.

BLUE SKIES

Ray Karnes painted our backdrops and did a splendid job of matching our fall foliage with his acrylic paints. The clouds were spray painted onto the skyboards by Mike Vivion, assisted by George Nelson. They made great use of some cloud templates, as is shown in fig. 14. Cloud colors were white and some shades of gray.

Speaking for everyone in the group, I hope you've enjoyed this project as much as we did bringing it to you. It was quite an experience. Now that I can start to enjoy some free time for the first time in more than a year, I think I'll get back to having some fun with my own trains! ♁

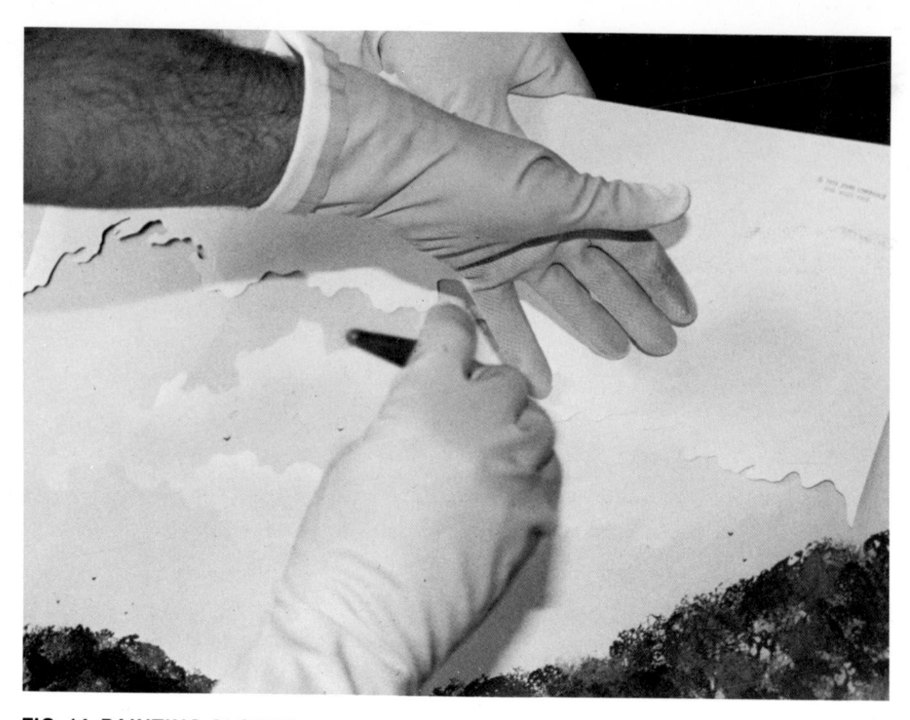

FIG. 14. PAINTING CLOUDS
The clouds were airbrushed onto the backdrops, using cardstock templates available from New London Industries, 8611 Norwich, San Antonio, TX 78217.